# Developing a Legal, Ethical, and Socially Responsible Mindset for Sustainable Leadership

Frank J. Cavico and Bahaudin G. Mujtaba

ILEAD Academy, LLC
Davie, Florida. United States of America
www.ileadacademy.com

Frank J. Cavico and Bahaudin G. Mujtaba, 2016. *Developing a Legal, Ethical, and Socially Responsible Mindset for Sustainable Leadership.*

Technical Production Manager: Bahaudin G. Mujtaba
Cover Design by: Cagri Tanyar

ISBN-13: 978-1-936237-07-4

ISBN-10: 1-936237-07-5

Subject Code & Description

BUS008000 - Business & Economics: Business Ethics
LAW036000 - Law: Ethics and Professional Responsibility
BUS094000 - Business & Economics: Green Business
PHI005000 - Philosophy: Ethics & Moral Philosophy

Printed in the United States of America, Davie, Florida.

> ☆ International ☆ <

# ILEAD ACADEMY
### Leadership Education and Associate Development Academy

# Dedication

This book is dedicated to those law-abiding, ethical, and socially responsible people and organizations around the globe!

# Table of Contents

# PREFACE

This book is about leadership and values, in particular the values of legality, morality, and social responsibility and their application in a modern global business environment. A business leader today must engage in sustainable leadership, which encompasses, in addition to making sound economic and financial decisions, acting legally based on the law, morally based on ethics, and also in a socially and environmentally responsible manner. Adherence to these values will result in a sustainable business, organization, community, society, and planet.

This book defines, differentiates, explains, and illustrates these values as well as their application to business. Although the focus of this book is on the business world, the values and principles explicated herein are relevant to leadership in the public sector and other professions. The "mindset" for sustainable leadership adduced and emphasized by the authors is for the leader contemplating a decision to ask three key questions: Is it legal? Is it moral? And what should a socially responsible firm or organization be doing for sustainable leadership?

Reflecting on these questions and acting in an appropriate manner based on legality, morality and social responsibility will lead to long-term value creation and competitive advantages - personal, business, organizational - and sustainable success.

# CHAPTER 1

## Introduction

Business is all about values. One core value is obviously the economic one, that is, business is expected to be profitable and to make money for the owners, shareholders, and investors. Business leaders, therefore, are expected to make sound financial and business decisions. However, business is further expected by society to achieve this economic value in conformity not only with the values of legality but also with the value of morality based on ethics. That is, business must act in a profitable, legal, and moral manner. Moreover, business leaders must deal with another important value – the societal expectation that business, as it grows and especially once it attains a certain size, wealth, and prominence, be "socially responsible." As such, above and beyond the responsibility to act legally and morally in the pursuit of profit is the notion of social responsibility, which typically today in a business context is called "corporate social responsibility" (CSR). The law defines legal accountability; ethics determines moral accountability; but ascertaining the definition, nature, extent of, and rationale for the value social responsibility emerges as an even more challenging task. Nevertheless, by acting in accord with economic, moral, and social responsibility values the business leader will achieve sustainability for his or her organization and will contribute to the sustainability of society. This book, therefore, takes a legal, philosophical, as well as practical approach, to explaining and illustrating these values in a modern-day, global, business environment. The notion of sustainability, as will be seen, has several components, including legal, ethical, spiritual, philanthropic, sustainability, reputational, and practical, all of which can at times be controversial and confusing (Yolles and Fink, 2014), but they will be explicated.

Global business leaders are likely to face many decisions that will impact themselves, their companies, employees, and colleagues, as well as their family members, local communities, and society in general. As such, it is incumbent upon business leaders, as well as community leaders, government regulators, and academics, to help business people to fully comprehend these values and their importance, so that they can act accordingly in the best interests of the business entity and all its relevant stakeholders including society as a whole. The authors thus hope that this book makes a modest contribution to inculcate such core values to the decision-making by business leaders.

The authors firmly believe that business leaders – whether entrepreneur, CEO, executive, officer, or manager- must act in a legal, ethical, and socially responsible manner. As such, business leaders in pursuing profits must obey the law, act for the greater good, treat all stakeholders with dignity and respect, and in a prudent manner be socially responsible by contributing to charities and participating in and supporting community and civic activities as well as engaging in sustainability activities. Acting in such a responsible way will require business leaders to be cognizant of various stakeholder interests as well as to seek to balance these at times conflicting constituencies in a fair and efficacious manner. This objective is a challenging one, indeed, but also a noble one. Yet the result will be the creation of long-term, sustainable value, not "merely" for the shareholders, but also for the employees, customers, communities, and all the stakeholders of the organization, including society as a whole and the future generations.

Capitalism and free markets are built on, as Adam Smith wisely stated long ago, a foundation of morality. The economy needs to be free to function, but the economy also needs rules to function correctly and effectively. And when the legal rules are not present or they are not clear, there is all the more need for ethics and socially responsible behavior. The idea is to create a sustainable form of capitalism, whereby acting in a legal, ethical, and socially responsible manner, as well as taking a long-term perspective, will produce profits for the shareholders but also long-term value for all the other stakeholders of the company. The task of business leaders, therefore, is to incorporate not only legal rules but also ethical, social responsibility, and stakeholder considerations into corporate values, mission statements, governance policy, and strategy, and to do so not "just" nationally but globally. Transparency, truthfulness, and trustworthiness have been, are, should be, and must be the hallmarks of business leadership and thus successful business; business leaders, therefore, have a moral obligation to be stewards and trustees of all the stakeholders of the organization. A true business leader must be keenly aware and engaged, must look ahead, must show the way, and must foresee the consequences of his or her company's actions on all the firm's stakeholders, including society as a whole. Business leaders must be aware that law, ethics, and social responsibility are all interconnected and underpin the economy, the free market system, and thus are essential for the sustainability of the organization, the economy, the political system, and the planet.

This book supplies a reminder, a rationale, and a guide for legal, ethical, and socially responsible behavior. Consequently, the authors hope that the book serves as a tool for true business leadership and business success, stakeholder responsibility, and organizational and societal sustainability. Capitalism and free markets, yes; but a system "regulated" and tempered by law, ethics, morality, and social responsibility; and thus an economic system with a "communitarian spirit" or, in the words of the Venetians long-ago (yet still quite true), a "communally controlled capitalism," as reflected in the spirit of Venetian motto and cardinal maxim - "All for the honor and profit of society."

Frank and Bahaudin

# CHAPTER 2

# Leadership and Values

Leadership is an important theme at the authors' university, Nova Southeastern University, and college of business, the H. Wayne Huizenga College of Business and Entrepreneurship, as it should be, of course, at any university, college, or school. Many students, particularly the graduate business students, will assume leadership roles in business as well as the public sector and professions (though this book focuses mainly on business context).

So, who is a leader and what are the components of successful and sustainable leadership. Initially, note that this book is not intended to be a leadership text; nevertheless, the authors would like to impart certain critical information on leadership in the context of the values addressed herein for business and leadership. *Leadership* is "the process of influencing an individual or a group of individuals while providing an environment where personal, professional, or organizational objectives can successfully be achieved"[1]. Leadership in the modern workplace is the process by which one person exerts influence over others in order to motivate and direct their behaviors toward the achievement of pre-determined goals and objectives[2]. The individual or person who exerts any form of influence that guides behavior toward a predetermined objective is considered to be a "leader"[3]. Of course, some of these leaders go "above and beyond" the exertion of influence and guidance of behavior; these few

---

1 MUJTABA, 2014, P. 92
2 CAVICO, MUJTABA, NONET, RIMANOCZY, AND SAMUEL, 2015.
3 MUJTABA, 2014

individuals are also able to achieve the final outcome by working with, and through, others in an efficient manner. As such, these few leaders are also good managers as they do the "right" things in the "right" manner.

Leadership and sustainability are interdependent concepts for long-term success and both can happen simultaneously as they are not mutually exclusive. Leaders who do not remain leaders for the long-term can be seen as merely "transactional" leaders as they would just use punishment and rewards to get what they want. However, such short-term leadership is not sustainable over time since once the penalty and rewards are gone, the expected behavior will also disappear. Furthermore, employees would perform as the transactional leader expects, not because they believe in the destination, objective, or outcome, but rather they comply to obtain the reward or to avoid a penalty. Consequently, people are likely to be compliant, at least temporarily, with such transactional leaders, but they will not necessarily have any commitment to the cause or goals.

Transformational or sustainable leadership is thus about effectiveness or doing the right things, and management is about efficiency or doing the right things right and with the least amount of resources in a speedy manner. As such, these sustainable or transformational leaders would also think like managers to make sure the process of how things get done is efficient in order to reduce the organization's "footprint on earth." Accordingly, effective leaders provide a long-term vision and guide others to the right direction for the right reasons, and not necessarily to earn any rewards and benefits. These sustainable and transformational leaders focus on people as well as task-oriented behaviors. First, *people-oriented* behaviors include showing mutual concern as well as trust and respect for subordinates. Second, *task-oriented* behaviors include defining and structuring work roles to ensure that everyone follows the stated rules in order to reach his or her performance capacity and meet the established standards.

The sustainable and transformational leaders must adapt their behaviors to fit a broad range of individuals and variables impacting their situations. Effective leadership is adapting one's behavior to the performance needs of others[4]. Effective leaders diagnose, adapt, and communicate based on the readiness of their followers in the workforce and other situational variables[5]. Dr. Paul Hersey defined a person's *readiness* level as one's ability and willingness to perform the task at hand and this definition considers two types of readiness: job and psychological[6]. Knowing a person's (follower's) readiness level and effectively adapting one's leadership behaviors to match the readiness level are important elements in making sure the job gets done successfully. Leaders can and do change their styles depending on with whom they are working. The situational leadership concept is based on the interactive interplay among direction (task behavior) provided by the leader, the socio-emotional support (relationship behavior) provided by the leader and the readiness of the follower to do the specific task that needs performing.

These sustainable or transformational leaders must learn the art of influencing others toward the right future vision. *Influencing* is defined as "the art of moving people to action toward a predetermined course or vision that is of value to everyone involved"[7]. Influencing requires the development of a long-term relationship or trust with the other party. Therefore, sustainable or transformational leadership

---

4 Hersey, Blanchard and Johnson, 2001
5 Hersey and Campbell, 2004
6 Mujtaba, 2014
7 Mujtaba, 2014, p. 81

requires *influencing* and persuading others, even over whom one has no position power or any direct authority[8].

In order to be an effective sustainable or transformational leader, one does not need any position power. For example, we know that managers often influence their employees to be great performers and model associates. Employees, on the other hand, influence one another, as well as their superiors and customers through their professionalism and rational explanations. Simply stated, influence is the ability to move others to action. Influencing allows individuals to get certain results from others without destroying their relationships. Effective influencing skills allow people to the get work done faster, as well as reduce conflict and stress, while demonstrating that one is a team-player and a flexible professional. All of these objectives lead to a more effective and sustainable work performance.

The sustainable and transformational leader empowers others to take action when he/she feels it is necessary. Through empowerment and collaboration the leader is able to tap into the employee's motivation. Effective sustainable and transformational leaders do not rely so much on position power as they depend on personal influence and power which comes through their relationships; and as such they align the individual's goals with those of the organization. Effective, sustainable, transformational leaders and managers become influential through training; as a result, their leadership effectiveness is raised to new levels through the appropriate and consistent use of their skills.

The business leader is expected to make sound business, personnel, and financial decisions. He or she must be proactive, that

---

8 HERSEY, BLANCHARD AND JOHNSON, 2001

is, be a "shaper" not a mere "reactor," and as such anticipate problems and challenges and then show the way to solve them, and finally solve or overcome them in an efficacious manner. A colleague of the authors, Professor Barry Barnes, succinctly sets forth the elements of successful leadership, to wit:

- Articulate an inspiring vision of the future.
- Lead by example. Walk the talk. And remember that you're always leading by example whether you realize it or not.
- Be trustworthy and create trust with followers.
- Have high expectations for followers. Setting the bar high will motivate followers to grow and achieve more...especially if it's linked to rewards.
- Challenge the process. Recognize that "the way we've always done things around here" won't always allow the organization to reach a common goal. As a result, be ready and willing to change the system and engage followers in the process of change.
- Adjust your style to meet follower needs. As followers improve performance, adjust your leadership style to move from telling followers what to do, to mentoring and persuading them, then to encouraging and facilitating their actions, and finally to simply entrusting them and monitoring their progress.
- Engage in strategic thinking and sustainability planning[9].

Barnes emphasizes that "in today's fast-changing world, there's a huge demand for capable and effective leaders all around the globe. In all modern organizations, we look for executives who can successfully lead it to a sustainable future. So what we need today are effective

---

[9] Barnes, 2013, paragraphs 1, 5

leaders at all levels of our organizations, whether they are executives, managers or simply informal leaders"[10].

The business leader today, therefore, must have "broad shoulders" as there are many challenges to business leaders, including the expectations that society has as to the proper conduct of business. The societal expectation is that business will act not "only" legally, but also morally; and then, when a business reaches a certain size and stature that business must also be more socially responsible. Business, moreover, is expected to help achieve sustainability. As a result, the business leader must be concerned with not only the economic and legal performance of the company, but also its moral and socially responsible performance, and ultimately its sustainability and societal sustainability.

Accordingly, a fundamental goal of this book is to make the reader keenly aware of societal expectations for entrepreneurs and business leaders and the concomitant responsibility of these leaders to ensure that each business acts legally, morally based on ethics, in a socially responsible manner, and contributes to overall societal and environmental sustainability. In addition to showing the way to proper business conduct a business leader must have the strength of character, conviction, and courage to object and dissent to proposed courses of action that may be, even if legal, immoral or socially irresponsible. Proper business leadership, therefore, necessitates that business leaders temper their pursuit of profit with the values of legality, morality, and social responsibility. In order for the company to maintain its leadership role, its leaders must be concerned about the impact its policies have on society, local communities, the environment, as well as future generations. The business leader thus

---

[10] Barnes, 2013, para. 1.

has the responsibility to create an organization, culture, and systems of for legal, moral, and socially responsible behavior. The goal is to make a positive contribution and have a positive impact for the organization and all its stakeholders, including society as a whole and future generations. Accordingly, strategic thinking and planning for sustainability are integral parts to successful business leadership. The "mindset" for the business leader, therefore, emerges essentially as a "three value drill"; that is, the business leader asking and answering these seminal questions: Is it legal, is it moral, and what would a socially responsible company or organization do? Yet what exactly do these key terms mean for leaders and their organizations?

# CHAPTER 3

# The Values of Legality, Morality, and Social Responsibility

We believe that one must be as precise as possible when engaging in analysis, particularly ethical analysis. Therefore, it is very important for a business leader, as well as academic, to look for, ascertain, and pay special attention to definitions and terms. To illustrate an area that will be more fully explicated in latter chapters, when one initially encounters the notion of social responsibility in a business context, one is confronted with some confusion due to a lack of an agreed-upon terminology and set of definitions. What is social responsibility? How does it differ from the law, ethics, and morality? What exactly do the terms "corporate social responsibility," "stakeholder values," "sustainability," "people, planet, and profits," "going green," and "socially responsible investing" mean? As such, if a business leader is going to understand what social responsibility is, and how it works in a modern global business environment, there must be some agreement on, and some insight into, the meaning and nature of the value of social responsibility, especially when juxtaposed with the values of legality, based on the law, and the value of morality, based on ethics.[11] These social responsibility definitions will be covered in detail in forthcoming chapters to this book. There is, therefore, a need for words, terms, and definitions with precise meaning. Definitions also can function, as per Socrates, as "definitional principles," that is, the "first principles" of reasoning to conclusions. If one defines terms

---

[11] Cavico, Mujtaba, Nonet, Rimanoczy, and Samuel, 2015.

carefully at the start, or knows the appropriate definitions, and one applies them consistently, one can draw conclusions deductively from these fundamental "first principles." The business leader, therefore, can use definitions and terms as principles to decide what to do in particular cases. Another key term to define is "values."

## A. Values

"Values," philosophically, are rankings or priorities that a person establishes for one's norms and beliefs. Values express what the chief end of life is, the highest good, and what things in life are worthwhile or desirable. Deeply held values can drive behavior. We use the term "value" or "values" when referring to legality, morality, and social responsibility. "Value" from a philosophical standpoint simply means something possesses worth. However, to complicate things philosophically as well as practically, values can be deemed "intrinsic" (sometimes called "terminal") and "instrumental" (also called "extrinsic"). A value is intrinsic if it is good and possesses worth in and of itself, like happiness or aesthetics (the appreciation of beauty). No further explanation or justification need be given for such an intrinsic value. Whereas a value is deemed instrumental if possesses worth not in and of itself but because it is a tool, instrument, or means to produce something else of value[12]. An example would be being nice and polite to people, even though one is a miserable and angry person. Why is one perhaps "forcing" oneself to be nice? Because being nice will lead to the making of friends, colleagues, allies, and teammates, and contented employees – all of which will benefit the "nice" (instrumentally so) person in the long-run. However, the best example of an instrumental value is money. What can you do with money in and of itself? It's "good for nothing,'" as the old song goes. But money is the means to buy lots of other things

---

[12] Cavico and Mujtaba, 2013

which then can bring happiness. So, who says that money can't buy happiness! We, consequently, concentrate on the instrumental value for business leaders and their companies by being regarded as legal, moral, and socially responsible individuals and businesses. So, instrumentally, what about the key values addressed in this book – legality, morality, and social responsibility – what is their worth?

## B. Legality

A significant value for the business community today is the value of legality, which is obviously based on the law. Actually, when making or contemplating a business decision, one of the first determinations to be made is whether the action is legal based on the law. The law is the set of public, universal commands that are capable of being complied with, generally accepted, and enforced by sanctions. Law describes the ways in which people are required to act in their relationships with others in an organized society. One purpose of the law is to keep people's ambitions, self-interest, and greed, especially in a capitalistic society, in check and in moderation[13]. Laws afford rights, but also impose duties. The law clearly possesses instrumental worth because one rightfully wants to be regarded as a legal actor and, concomitantly, one and one's firm does not want to be sued civilly or prosecuted criminally (and perhaps be convicted and imprisoned) for violating the law.

Today, obviously, there are many, many laws that govern and regulate business which the business leader must be aware. To illustrate, in the United States there exists constitutions, statutes, administrative rules and regulations, case law, and executive orders. Moreover, the U.S., like many other countries has a federal system of government, so there are national (called "federal law" in the U.S.)

---

[13] Cavico and Mujtaba, 2013, 2014.

and state and local law. Furthermore, in the United States, certain statutory laws, for example Civil Rights laws and Anti-trust laws have extraterritorial effect, that is, they can apply to the employees of U.S. companies doing business overseas. There are also the "domestic" laws in the host countries where one does business; and there are international laws, treaties, and conventions[14].

Nevertheless, despite the prevalence of the law, the business leader must be aware of "moral gaps" in the law; that is, the countries and localities where there is no law, weak law, or unenforced law (perhaps due to bribery). Furthermore, there are "vague" lines the law draws, for example, the "line" between a "good will gift" to a foreign government official and an illegal bribe pursuant to the Foreign Corrupt Practices Act. Another example of a vague line is the distinction the law makes between inside or insider trading which clearly is illegal, and trading on inside information which *may* be legal. The law also affords options for acting, for example, closing facilities, moving overseas or to another state and doing the concomitant "down-sizing" (such as in the case of a big merger)[15].

Despite the importance and prevalence of the law, especially laws regulating business, it is not a principal purpose of this book to be a business law or government regulation of business text. Nevertheless, the law must be juxtaposed with yet differentiated from morality and ethics as well as social responsibility. And, most importantly, the reader must be made cognizant of the fact that there are many moral gaps in the law, meaning that an action might be legal but immoral based on ethics. Attorneys, of course, will be ready, willing, and able to advise business people (with their concomitant legal fees, naturally) on the legality of their actions. Yet, who will

---

[14] Cavico and Mujtaba, 2014
[15] Ibid

advise the business leader as to the morality of his or her actions? Any examination of morality perforce brings one into the realm of ethics, which is a branch of philosophy.

## C. Morality and Ethics

Philosophy is the study and analysis of such deeply problematic and fundamental question, such as the nature of reality, thought, conduct, and morality. Ethics *is* a branch of philosophy. Moral philosophy is the philosophical study of morality; it is the application of philosophy to moral thinking, moral conduct, and moral problems. Moral philosophy encompasses various theories that prescribe what is good for people and what is bad, what constitutes right and wrong, and what one ought to do and ought not to do. Moral philosophy offers ethical theories that provide a theoretical framework for making, asserting, and defending a moral decision. There is not one determinate set of ethical theories. Moral philosophy embraces a range of ethical perspectives and spends a great deal of time in analyzing the differences among these ethical views. Moral philosophy attempts to establish logical thought processes that will determine if an action is right or wrong and seeks to find principled ethical criteria by which to distinguish good conduct from bad conduct[16].

"Ethics" is the theoretical study of morality. Ethical theories are moral philosophical undertakings that contain bodies of formal, systematic, and ethical principles that are committed to the view that an asserted ethical theory can determine how one should morally think and act. Ethics is the sustained and reasoned attempt to determine what is morally right or wrong. Ethics is used to test the moral correctness of beliefs, practices, and rules. Ethics necessarily

---

[16] Cavico and Mujtaba, 2013.

involves an effort both to define what is meant by morality and to justify the way of acting and living that is being advocated. Ethics proceeds from a conviction that moral disagreements and conflicts are resolvable rationally. The purpose of ethics is to develop, articulate, and justify principles and techniques that can be used in specific situations where a moral determination must be made about a particular action or practice. When a decision involves a moral component, the decision necessarily encompasses moral rules and ethical principles[17].

"Morals" are beliefs or views as to what is right or wrong or good or bad. Moral norms are standards of behavior by which people are judged and that require, prohibit, or allow specific types of behavior. Moral rules are action-guiding or prescriptive statements about how people ought to behave or ought not to behave. Moral standards enable resolution of disputes by providing acceptable justification for actions. If one bases a decision on a moral rule, and if the moral rule is based on and derived from an agreed-upon ethical principle, the decision should be publicly acceptable. It then is a reasoned ethical conclusion directed toward what one ought or ought not to do. Morality, therefore, properly and accurately should be understood as a development of the ethical. Morality and ethics, consequently, are different from the much more modern notion of social responsibility.

## D. Social Responsibility

First and foremost, social responsibility is *neither* a branch of philosophy *nor* part of ethics; social responsibility is *not* an ethical theory, *not* an ethical principle, and *not* a means to determine morals, morality, or moral precepts.

---

[17] Cavico and Mujtaba, 2013.

Social responsibility, however, now is not "just" an "academic" matter for business school students, or "merely" an "issue" for social activists; rather, social responsibility is also a very real and practical concern for the global business leader, executive, manager and entrepreneur. Admittedly, in certain cases, social responsibility concerns may be more difficult for business people, who are primarily focused on economic issues, to discern and to handle. Moreover, there may be conflicts as various constituencies make conflicting demands. Nonetheless, business leaders are expected to recognize competing stakeholder interests, to provide balance among legitimate competing claims, and, as emphasized, to devise practical, legal, ethical, socially responsible, as well as mutually beneficial solutions. Business leaders very well may have to convince certain stakeholders, such as the shareholders, that it is in their long-term self-interest to accept some short-term financial sacrifice, say in the form of company socially and environmentally responsible efforts in the local community, in order to produce long-term greater financial gains.

## E. Sustainable Leadership

The expectations today are that business leaders and business must act legally, morally, and in a socially responsible manner. That is the "mindset" – the "three value drill" for business leaders. And that mindset is the way to achieve sustainability; and business leaders must show the way. Consequently, the challenge for business leaders today is to fulfill these expectations and to meet these challenges. The principal objective of this book, therefore, is to help the reader act in conformity with these values and achieve success. And the rationale for adherence to these values (though not without cost, effort, and time) will be sustainability. That is, the business leader will be able to achieve success and will be able to *sustain* that success for himself or herself, their companies and organizations, their communities, for society as a whole, and for future generations. The basic formula of this book, which will be further explicated in the forthcoming chapters, for an organization with a sound economic business model is this: the value of *legality* + the value of *morality/ethics* + the value of *social responsibility* + taking responsibility for environmental and operational *sustainability (as a means)* = Sustainable Leadership *(as an ends)*.

The Sustainable Leadership Model, presented in Figure 3.1, indicates the relationship among the core values explicated in this book and illustrates how adherence to these values culminates in successful and sustainable leadership of the business or organization.

Figure 3.1 – Sustainable Leadership Model

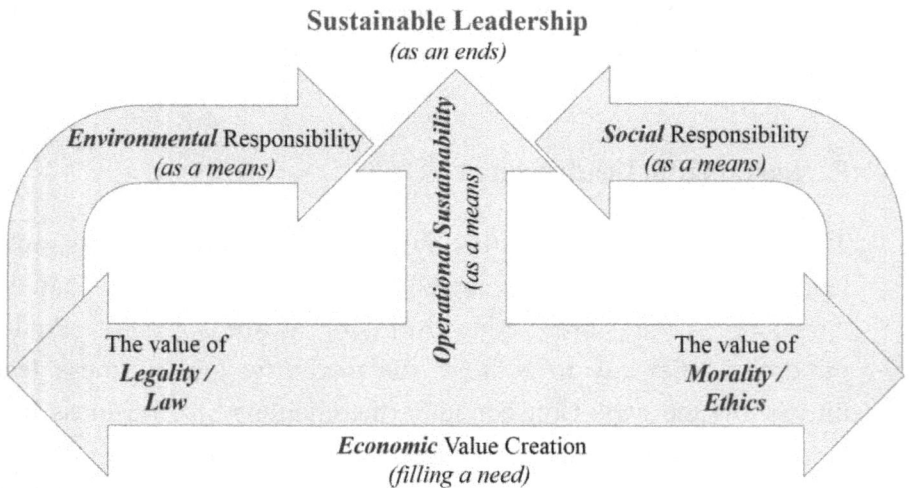

**Sustainable Leadership**
*(as an ends)*

*Environmental* Responsibility
*(as a means)*

*Social* Responsibility
*(as a means)*

*Operational Sustainability*
*(as a means)*

The value of
*Legality /*
*Law*

The value of
*Morality /*
*Ethics*

*Economic* Value Creation
*(filling a need)*

Modern firms and leaders must become stewards of their firms and their local communities if they are to remain competitive and sustainable over time by meeting the needs of their customers and other stakeholders in value creation. Sustainable leadership is no longer a "nice thing" to do, but rather such leadership is a "must" objective for modern local and global corporations. We provide a comprehensive model for "Sustainable Leadership." The model encompasses having a good, "solid" economic and business foundation together with practicing the values of legality, morality and ethics, and social responsibility. Moreover, social responsibility includes charitable and civic-minded endeavors and also environmental protection and conservation efforts in the community as well as in business operations.

Many modern thinkers and experts offer similar suggestions for effective and sustainable leadership. To illustrate, according to Mohrman, O'Toole, and Lawler (2015), stewardship demands a good understanding, as well as the acceptance, of each firm's interdependence with society and the general environment where the organization does business. Their book, entitled *"Corporate Stewardship: Achieving Sustainable Effectiveness,"* discusses how modern business leaders must embrace stewardship in the current market while balancing stewardship with making a fair profit yet without any detrimental impact for the environment or future generations. These authors provide leading philosophies and approaches in sustainability along with practical guidance on how modern leaders and their organizations can effectively deal with the challenges of complex interdependencies among firms, communities, society, and the environment.

Mohrman, O'Toole, and Lawler (2015), therefore, emphasize that it is critical for modern firms and leaders to "grow" their profits in a responsible, ethical, and sustainable manner. Accordingly, business leaders as stewards must not only make good use of their existing resources, but they must also leave sufficient resources as well as improved assets and means for use by future generations. Modern business leaders, managers, executives, and entrepreneurs thus must think and act as stewards of their organizations as well the social and physical environments in order to be successful and to remain sustainable over time.

# CHAPTER 4

# Ethics, Applied Business Ethics, and Morality

Moral questions perforce bring one into the realm of ethics. There is, and this point is emphasized throughout the book, a societal expectation today that business will act not merely legally but also morally. Note that from a philosophic standpoint morality and ethics are distinct concepts. Morality is based on ethics which is a branch of philosophy. Morals and morality are technically the conclusion as to what is right or wrong or good or bad or moral or immoral. And how does one arrive at these moral conclusions? One reaches morality by reasoning from ethics. As such, ethics are the intellectual framework, the theories, and the principles that one uses to reason to moral decisions, morality, morals. The discerning reader, therefore, must make that critical distinction between morality and ethics. As such, the ethics presented in this book is not a didactic or "preachy" or sermonizing type of ethics, but rather an exercise in logic and reasoning from ethical theories and principles to morality[18] . So, the next ethics question emerges: What ethical theories and principles?

The authors in this book succinctly deal with the four main ethical theories in Western Civilization and demonstrate how to apply them to determine if business, even if acting legally, is acting morally. Now, of course, Western Civilization is not the only one, but it is the one that the authors and likely the readers of this book are most familiar with. Moreover, the four ethical theories chosen for explication in this book are secular-based one. As such, there is no

---

[18] Cavico and Mujtaba, 2013

religious component to the book. The reasons are several: first, not everyone "has religion," and certainly not everyone has the same religion. However, everyone (presumably) has reason; and thus can reason from secular ethical theories and principles to morality. So, in this book the readers are being exposed to secular, Western-based ethics. Specifically, the four secular-based ethical theories that will be discussed in this book are: Ethical Egoism, Ethical Relativism, Utilitarianism, and Kantian ethics.

## A. Ethical Egoism

Ethical Egoism should be a very acceptable and accommodating ethical theory for anyone, especially a business person, because pursuant to that theory it is moral to advance self-interest, to prosper, and to make money. An action that supports or advances one's self-interest is a moral one; and conversely an action that impedes or is harmful to one's self-interest is immoral. However, the "enlightened" ethical egoists, such as Adam Smith, would counsel to take a long-term perspective as to maximizing self-interest; and thus one should be willing to undergo some short-term expense, sacrifice, and effort in order to advance one's self-interest in the long-term. As such, promulgating a corporate code of ethics, having an "open-door" policy, and otherwise treating the employees fairly and well, although initially taking time, effort, and money, are the right things to do, the smart things to do, and thus are the moral things to do. The beneficial result will be good employee relations, fewer turnover problems; and more productive employees; and thus the self-interest of the firm will be advanced. Also, even if one has a big ego as well as a lot of power, the ethical egoists would advise that it is best to treat people well, and not necessarily because one loves them, or even likes them, but it will usually inure to one's benefit to treat people well and make them colleagues, allies, and part of the "team." Recall the instrumental value of being nice!

## B. Ethical Relativism

The second ethical theory is Ethical Relativism. "When in Rome, do as the Romans," as the old saying goes. Pursuant to this ethical theory, an action is moral if a society believes it to be moral. Consequently, societal norms become the standard for morality. All one has to do is to ascertain the moral norms of a particular society and adopt them and conform, and one will be acting morally. So, if the Italians and French use nudity in their advertising campaigns and have no moral qualms about such marketing, well, "When in Rome...," (perhaps literally), you too can use nudity, assuming you are an Ethical Relativist, of course. With this ethical theory, one does need to be a philosopher or an ethicist here; rather, one just needs to have sharp "eyes and ears" to ascertain what the "local" moral norms and precepts are. Of course, one needs to determine what the "society" is first, which can be challenging in a heterogeneous society. However, just because a practice is deemed to be moral in a society the business person must be aware that there may be a superseding law that makes it illegal (for example, a moral, pursuant to ethical relativism, "good will gift" to a foreign government official, which is an accepted practice in the host country; yet a "gift" that the U.S government deems to be an illegal bribe under the Foreign Corrupt Practices Act).

## C. Utilitarianism

The third ethical theory is Utilitarianism, which is a relatively modern ethical theory created by the English philosophers and social reformers, Jeremy Bentham and John Stuart Mill. The core principle to this ethical theory is: "An action is moral if it produces the greatest amount of good for the greatest number of people." Accordingly, this ethical theory is a consequentialist ethical theory; one must predict consequences; one must ascertain whether the consequences are good or bad, cause pleasure or pain, happiness or dissatisfaction; and then one must measure and weigh consequences. If there are predominant good consequences, the action is a moral action; and if there are predominant negative consequences the action is immoral. But it must be emphasized that even if an action is moral there still may be some pain, which means that "ends can justify means"; yet everyone got "counted," everyone's pleasure and pain was registered based on this egalitarian ethical theory. Of course, the Utilitarians would say to try to find actions that minimize any pain, and hopefully eliminate it in a "win-win" type of scenario. As a practical bit of advice, we suggest that when predicting consequences one should make those determinations within discrete stakeholder groups, as that approach would "channel" and thus make more manageable the predictive aspect of this ethical theory; and many readers of this book should be familiar with stakeholder analysis too. For example, a big mergers, like the Staples-Office Depot or Kraft-Heinz mergers, the consequences of the merger should be examined in the context of the following key stakeholder groups: shareholders, employees, unions, consumers/customers, suppliers and distributors, local communities, government, competition, and society as a whole. Utilitarianism thus has several positive attributes: people should be used to its integral element of predicting consequences (as they do it for themselves); the theory takes a broad approach to ascertaining morality; all people and stakeholders directly and indirectly affected by an action are examined; everyone gets "counted"; there are no special and privileged people; everyone's pleasure and pain is registered; and thus the Utilitarian theory is a very egalitarian one. However, one big problem can arise when the "counting" is done since there may be a predominance of good consequences caused by the action, which means it is moral pursuant to this ethical theory; but there still may be some lesser bad, and perhaps very "painful," consequences to a minority of people affected by the action. Nevertheless, despite some negative consequences the action is moral pursuant to Utilitarianism.

## D. Kantian Ethics

Finally, the fourth ethical theory is Kantian ethics, which is also a relatively modern ethical theory but one diametrically opposed to Utilitarianism. Regarding Utilitarianism, Kant condemned that ethical theory as being immoral because it could morally justify pain, suffering, and exploitation. That is, the problem of the "ends justifying the means." So, Kant declared that one should disregard consequences in making moral determinations. Thus, as the discerning reader can plainly see, a major problem emerges in Western ethics due to the conflict between the two modern ethical theories. So, how does Kant determine morality? Morality is based on a formal test that Kant called Categorical Imperative. "Categorical" because, according to Kant, this is the supreme, absolute, and only test for morality; and "Imperative" because at times one must compel oneself to be moral, that is, to do what one's reason tells one is the "right" thing to do, even though there may be some negative consequences to one personally (for example, "blowing the whistle" on one's polluting company). Have a "good will," declared Kant. That is, be morally strong, have a good moral character, do your duty – not necessarily to the law or to the state – but your duty to yourself - do what your mind tells you is the moral thing to do, regardless of consequences. Overcome fear, lust, greed, envy, an overarching ambition, go perhaps "above and beyond" the law, and do the "right" thing. So, what is the "right" thing to do pursuant to the Categorical Imperative?

Since Kant wants one to be very sure that one is acting morally, within the Categorical Imperative there are three main tests for morality that one must apply to the action itself to determine its morality; and all three tests must be passed; all these tests are interrelated and some Kantian scholars actually say that there are only two main tests (but we will save that issue for the philosophy department). The first is the Universal Law test. Under this test one must ask if the action one is contemplating would be one that one, hypothetically, would be willing to make into a universal "law." That is, for example, take the actions of cheating, lying, and stealing. Would one want to live in a society where the moral norm is that it is permissible to cheat, lie, and steal? A rational person would of course say no; and would not want those actions to be done to him or her; and thus the actions are immoral. Now, people do cheat, lie, and steal, and Kant admits that, but he condemns them as "parasites" on an otherwise moral system where the vast majority of people do not cheat, lie, or steal. The second is the Kingdom of Ends test which holds that an action is immoral, regardless of consequences, if it is disrespectful and demeaning to anyone, if it treats anyone like an instrument or thing or mere means (even to achieve a greater good). Since a person knows that he or she is a human being, a worthwhile person deserving of dignity and respect, one thus should reason that other people feel the same too. In essence, for Kant, the core principle is for all people to treat all others with dignity and respect, and thus all will live in the Kingdom of Ends wherein all are treated as worthwhile ends and not as mere means. The third main part to the Categorical Imperative is the Agent-Receiver test (which actually is the Golden Rule made secular by Kant). Pursuant to this ethical principle, Kant would say to consider the contemplated action, but if one did not know if one would be the agent, that is, the giver of the action, or the receiver of the action, would one be willing to have that action done. So, using the Categorical Imperative and the example of the merger, if the merger produces greater good overall it is moral under Utilitarianism, but if any stakeholder group is disrespected or demeaned the merger is immoral. And to take a more dramatic illustration, what does one say morally about a legal but exploitative "sweatshop"? It certainly produces a lot of good inexpensive products, and thus good in the form of money for a lot of stakeholders, and perhaps more good than bad, which would be enough for a Utilitarian conclusion of "moral" for the 'sweatshop," but what would Kant say after seeing the conditions of the "sweatshop" - the age of the young workers, their gender and perhaps harassment, their wages, the lack of safety standards? One plainly can reason to an opposite Kantian moral conclusion. That, in a "nutshell," is the moral conflict in Western ethics.

## E. The Ethical Challenge and Rationale for Business Leaders

To determine morality, at least at a philosophical level, one needs ethics, and the philosophic ethics of the sort that is delineated herein. The discerning reader, therefore, must know, or reflect a little on philosophy (and, regarding philosophy, the authors feel that "a little goes a long ways") in the form of ethics. The four ethical theories briefly presented in this book are the four major, secular ethical theories. So, without being "culturally imperialistic, the authors would submit that the ethical challenge for the business leader today is to strive to engage in actions that advance the self-interest of the firm (Ethical Egoism), that are culturally competent (Ethical Relativism), and that achieve the greater good (Utilitarianism), especially by aiming for "win-win" scenarios for all stakeholders, *but* to do actions that do *not* demean or disrespect any stakeholders (Kantian Ethics). Again, meeting this challenge may take foresight, time, effort, and money. Yet, why bother, particularly if one is already acting legally? No one is going to sue you or your firm for acting immorally (assuming you are not violating any law).

Consequently, why be moral? The rationale for acting morally, the authors submit, goes back to the first ethical theory - Ethical Egoism. That is, acting morally will inure to one's own long-term advancement and self-interest as well as that of one's company or organization they are regarded, and rightfully so, as not only legal but also moral. To illustrate, a recent study on leadership and character reported in the *Harvard Business Review*[19] asked the question if highly principled leaders and their organizations perform especially well. And the answer was "yes." The study revealed that principled CEOs who have high marks for "character," in the form of

---

[19] 2015.

possessing integrity and fulfilling responsibilities along with demonstrating forgiveness and compassion, lead their firms to better financial performance than CEOs with low marks for character. Accordingly, the role of a leader includes educating others as to their own long-term self-interest; that is, the business leader must show the way (perhaps to top management, the board of directors, and the shareholders) that acting morally will benefit the business in the long-run and contribute to its own sustainability. Yet there is an even greater societal expectation and thus more responsibility, even above and beyond morality and ethics, to be thrust on the "broad shoulders" of the business leader.

# CHAPTER 5

# Corporate Social Responsibility: A Strategic Approach

Another challenge for business leaders today is that business is expected to act not only legally and morally but also in a socially responsible manner. This societal expectation of being socially responsible is thus above and beyond the law and even morality/ethics. Business, therefore, is expected to be a "socially responsible" one and a good "corporate citizen" (even though there may be neither a legal nor a moral obligation to do so)[20]. The World Business Council for Sustainable Development similarly defines social responsibility in a business context as a company's continuing commitment to act legally and morally and also to contribute to the economic development of society while improving the quality of life of their employees and their families as well as the local community and society as a whole.

One dilemma when dealing with "social responsibility" is to precisely define the term. Legality is based on laws (though vague laws at times); morality is based on theories and principles (though perhaps even more vague); but social responsibility is based on current explanations of the term. Typically, as will be seen in this chapter, the definition is a very broad one; and consequently "social responsibility" means that business is involved in charitable organizations and activities and philanthropy as well as civic and

---

[20] Cavico, 2014.

community activities. But social responsibility in the broad sense contains a sustainability element, that is, sustainability as a *means* in the form of environmental protection activities and "going green" endeavors, such as solar and wind projects and saving water. One thus sees under the rubric of social responsibility such "sustainability" slogans and notions as the "3 P's: People, Planet, Profits" and the "Triple Bottom Line" (Economic Prosperity, Environmental Stewardship, and Social Responsibility). Sustainability as a "means" and also as an "ends" will be addressed in forthcoming chapters of this book.

## A. The Nature of Social Responsibility

What exactly is the "social responsibility" of business? Does a corporation have a social obligation to take care of the poor, educate the public, give to charity, and fund cultural programs? Does a business have to engage in environmental protection and "green" activities? Social projects and social welfare in the United States as well as protecting the environment traditionally have been viewed as the appropriate domain of government, not of business. Business, of course, is taxed and such taxes may be used for such social purposes. The traditional purpose of business as viewed in the U.S., moreover, is the profitable production and distribution of goods and services, not social welfare or environmental protection. Yet, today, the topic of the social responsibility of business is raised by many people and groups who expect business to act in a "socially responsible" manner. Consequently, business leaders are now compelled to concern themselves with the "social" dimension of business activities.

The concept of the social responsibility for business was first introduced by the prominent scholar, Adolf Berle, in his 1932 text, co-authored with Gardner Means, *The Modern Corporation and*

*Private Property*, wherein the notions of community and stakeholder interest, service to the public, "trusteeship" to non-shareholder constituencies, stabilization and continuance of business, as well as a broader social understanding of corporations, were first raised. However, Berle did not elaborate how the corporation should determine what these broader stakeholder and community interests are or how it should be advanced; but nonetheless scholars claim that Berle commenced the debate over corporate social responsibility.

Today, however, the debate appears to be mainly settled; and consequently business leaders must take a broad stakeholder approach to business decision-making. A constituency or stakeholder approach to corporate social responsibility requires management to balance shareholder and non-shareholder interests. Shareholders, as owners of the firm, are obviously an important stakeholder group, but other non-shareholder groups, like the employees, local community, and the environment, must be considered too. Maximizing profit, particularly short-term profit, solely for the shareholders, is no longer considered to be socially responsible for business.

Accordingly, what is the "social responsibility" of business today? The term at a basic philanthropic level may be defined as a business taking an active party in the social causes, charities, and civic life of one's community and society. For example, Facebook founder, Mark Zuckerberg, donated $100 million to help fix schools in Newark, New Jersey. Newman's Own is a private sector company praised for its philanthropic mission since it donates all of its profits and royalties after taxes for charitable and educational purposes.

However, corporate social responsibility (CSR) certainly can be more than "mere" philanthropy. The emphasis can be placed on creating shared value; that is, business leaders making decisions that are valuable for the business and its owners, but which also provide a meaningful benefit for society. A prime example would be Toyota's development of the Prius hybrid automobile. The objective is to make money (legally of course) but also benefit society by fulfilling specific societal needs or solving societal problems.

Maggins and Tsaklanganos[21] underscore two important aspects of social responsibility: first, its multifaceted interpretation; and second, its relationship to sustainability. They[22] reflect that there are "various definitions" of corporate social responsibility, but "most share the theme of engaging in economically sustainable business activities that go beyond legal requirements in order to protect the well-being of employees, communities, and the environment." The objective is to simultaneously produce economic value for the company, but also value for society as a whole by helping to solve societal needs, particularly by improving the lives of the people (and potential consumers), who live in the communities where the company does business. Andre[23] notes that corporate social responsibility is an "umbrella concept used in the fields of management, business ethics, political theory, and legal philosophy," which is used to describe the responsibilities of the corporation to constituencies beyond the shareholder group, and which "is often used interchangeably with such terms as corporate citizenship, stakeholder management, and social enterprise".

---

[21] 2012.
[22] Maggins and Tsaklanganos, 2012, p. 662.
[23] 2012, p. 134.

## B. CSR in the U.S. and Globally

A corporation, of ccurse, is a profit-making entity that exists in a competitive environment, and thus may be limited in its ability to solve a multitude of social problems particularly at the expense of the owners of the corporation – the shareholders. Where are the philanthropic guidelines for corporate contributions and improvements? How should a corporation's resources be allocated, and exactly to whom, to what extent, and in what priorities? What is the proper balance between shareholder and stakeholder interests? If a corporation unilaterally or too generously engages in social betterment, it may place itself at a disadvantage compared to other less socially responsible business entities. Being socially responsible costs money, and such efforts cut into profits. In a highly competitive market system, corporations that are too socially responsible may lessen their attractiveness to investors or simply may price themselves out of the market. "Charity begins at home" was the very prudent social responsibility conclusion in a *Newsweek* article[24] regarding the saga of THE socially responsible firm – Ben & Jerry's, which has long been known and lauded for its civic, community, and environmental efforts. Mickels[25] notes that "many people consider Ben & Jerry's as the first 'socially responsible' company by introducing the concept of improving the environment as a second bottom line." Yet the company may have been *too* socially responsible and consequently neglectful of basic business concerns. Ultimately, the original former "hippies" Ben Cohen and Jerry Greenfield of Ben & Jerry's sold their interests in their company in 2000 to global consumer products giant, Unilever, which carried on the social responsibility activities of the brand to a degree; but, as *Newsweek* reported, several company franchisees, primarily small

---

[24] Smalley, 2007.
[25] 2009, p. 274.

entrepreneurs, are suing the firm, contending that Ben & Jerry's treated them unfairly, for example, by not providing adequate training and assistance, by giving wholesale price "breaks" to large buyers, such as Wal-Mart and Costco, thereby undercutting them, by not sufficiently marketing their franchises, and by misrepresenting average gross sales for stores. Unilever is denying the allegations, but is working with its franchisees by waiving royalty fees, renegotiating store leases, and increasing marketing support. A representative from Unilever stated that it is an "ethic" of Ben & Jerry's to treat its franchisees well, which is all "well and good," but *Newsweek* posited that the lesson to be learned in this episode for "socially responsible" companies is that "Charity begins at home." There is a further problem in expecting the corporation to take on the betterment of the "general welfare." Corporations already possess great power, and corporate executives neither are the elected representatives of the people nor are answerable directly to the general public. Corporate executives lack the mandate that a democratic society grants to those who are supposed to promote the general welfare. Government officials, elected by the people, rightfully are thought of as the social guardians of the people.

The topic of social responsibility nonetheless has emerged as such a critical one for global business too. Of course, the nature and practice of social responsibility likely will be different from country to country, industry to industry, and business to business because of varying local circumstances, especially the demands (or lack thereof) of governments and other stakeholders as well as differing societal norms.

There are many examples of corporate social responsibility globally. Good examples are Nokia's and Ericsson's efforts to bring mobile communications technology to the developing world. Another example would be the Coca-Cola's company's efforts to provide clean water to parts of the developing world, which Coke also hopes to promote goodwill, boost local economies, and broaden its customer base. As noted, Royal Caribbean Cruise Company is teaming up with a Haitian non-profit organization to build a primary school, which is located on land the company leases from the government as a stop for its ships in the port town of Labadee. Wal-Mart is now selling online handicrafts made by women artisans in developing countries, such as dresses made in Kenya and jewelry from Guatemala and Thailand. Over 500 items from 20,000 female artisans are being offered for sale, which certainly will help the female artisans but also improve the company's global image. Two more examples of global corporate social responsibility are as follows: The Norwegian company, Yara International, the world's largest chemical fertilizer company, has sponsored public/private partnerships to develop storage, transportation, and port facilities in parts of Africa with significant untapped agricultural potential, thereby developing local agriculture, providing jobs and improved incomes for farmers, and at the same time benefiting the company through an increased demand for its fertilizer products. The Nestle Company is working to improve milk production in certain regions of India, by investing in well drilling, refrigeration, veterinary medicine, and training, thereby significantly increasing output and enhancing product quality, certainly beneficial to the company, and at the same time allowing the company to pay higher prices for farmers and their employees, resulting in a higher standard of living for the local community.

The reasons for the extent of corporate social responsibility globally are manifold. First, companies realize that they need to respond to large scale social problems before they become a threat to business. Second, on a more positive note, human resources experts contend that solutions to major social problems can increasingly be viewed as new sources of business opportunities. That is, providing goods and services to the people of developing nations may be a way to enter into potentially vast markets of consumers. Similarly, "going green" and investing in environmentally "friendly" technology may be a way for companies to initially establish themselves in potentially highly profitable energy sectors. Similarly, Millon[26] calls for a corporate social responsibility approach globally for the following reasons: "For transnational corporations doing business in developed countries, sustainability may require investment in community-level infrastructure development projects, technological innovation, education, and health care. As these investments lead to greater productivity and better product quality, workers and producers can earn higher incomes, allowing the local population to enjoy a higher standard of living".

The United Nations now has a business initiative on corporate social responsibility, called the United Nations Global Compact, wherein companies can join and thus voluntarily agree to make improvements in human rights, labor relations, and the environment, as well as combating corruption. The United Nations also has a Global Reporting Initiative where companies can report their social responsibility and sustainability efforts. The World Bank, moreover, now has an Internet course on social responsibility, called "Corporate Social Responsibility and Sustainable Competitiveness," offered by its educational and training division, the World Bank Institute. The corporate social responsibility course is designed for "high-level" private sector managers, government officials and regulators, practitioners, academics, and journalists. One major purpose to the course is to provide a "conceptual framework" for improving the business environment to support social responsibility efforts and practices by corporations and business. The course is also designed to

---

[26] 2011, p. 531.

assist companies to formulate a social responsibility strategy based on "integrity and sound values" as well as one with a long-term perspective. By being socially responsible, declares the World Bank, businesses not only will accrue benefits, but also civil society as a whole will benefit from the "positive contributions" of business to society.

Although it is beyond the scope of this book to discuss in detail the World Bank's very laudable corporate social responsibility educational effort, a few key elements in the course must be addressed. First and foremost, as the World Bank points out, correctly so, there is no single, commonly accepted, definition of the critical term "corporate social responsibility." Nonetheless, the World Bank offers its definition, stating that corporate social responsibility generally refers to: 1) "a collection of policies and practices linked to the relationship with key stakeholders, values, compliance with legal requirements, and respect for people, communities and the environment; and 2) the commitment of business to contribute to sustainable development." The World Bank also explains the key term "Corporate Citizenship," which is "the concept of the corporation as a citizen" and which is a term often used when referring to corporate social responsibility. As a matter of fact, the World Bank notes, again quite correctly, that the terms "Corporate Social Responsibility" and "Corporate Citizenship" are at times used interchangeably. The World Bank, moreover, in order to fully explicate corporate social responsibility, indicates several material components to that concept, to wit: 1) environmental protection, 2) labor security, 3) human rights, 4) community involvement, 5) business standards, 6) marketplace, 7) enterprise and economic development, 8) health protection, 9) education and leadership development, and 10) human disaster relief. The World Bank offers several decision-making frameworks for companies to plan, implement, and measure social responsibility. An important part of the World Bank course is a segment, eminently practical for the business leader, called "Benefits of Corporate Social Responsibility." There are many reasons why it pays for companies, both large businesses and small and medium enterprises to be socially responsible and thus to be conscious about the interests and values of key stakeholders. Customers will "reward" or "punish" businesses by either buying or not buying their products based on the perceived social responsibility performance (or lack thereof) of the companies. Other reasons for being a socially responsible firm are as follows: 1) obtaining a "social license" to operate from key stakeholders; 2) ensuring "sustainable competitiveness," 3) creating new business opportunities, 4) attracting and retaining quality investors and business partners, 5) securing cooperation from local communities, 6) avoiding difficulties due to socially irresponsible behavior, 7) obtaining government support, and 8) building "political capital." These reasons clearly make the "business case" for the business leader to show the way to positioning his or her firm as a socially responsible one.

In the context of India, though certainly appropriate to other developing countries, Kumar, Kuberudu, and Krishna[27] offer the following recommendations for "socially responsible" businesses: 1) create and nurture an "eco-friendly environment" within and outside the organization; 2) adopt poor, needy, and "sleepy" villages and bring them into inclusive growth by supplying "eco-friendly" projects; 3) wage a "war" on bribery and corruption; 4) control pollution, including "social pollution," and help build a "healthy society"; 5) provide assistance when natural calamities occur; 6) develop the "highest ethical standards" with "transparency" as the "watch word"; 7) avoid deceptive and exaggerated advertisement, be

---

[27] 2011, pp. 10-11.

restrained by "general social acceptability" regarding advertising, and do not exploit women in advertising; 8) offer financial scholarships and financial assistance to meritorious students; assistance in education and vocational training; and adopt schools, providing for their growth and management. These social responsibility activities will naturally help companies fulfill their legal and moral obligations, but also will result in a more stable and flourishing society, the success and survival of the organization, and an increase in profits. Plainly, there is a relationship between the well-being of an organization and the good will of the people in a society. Thus, it "pays" to be socially responsible – domestically and globally; doing good can result in doing well.

## C. The Strategic Rationale for Social Responsibility

As emphasized, another strategic factor to success and sustainability now has emerged in the present business environment – social responsibility. The idea is not "only" to make profits but then to "give back" to the community by means of civil, social, and environmental efforts. Yet a strategic approach to social responsibility would combine profits and social activism; that is, the smart and social company will deliver products and services that naturally are profitable but that also serve society, for example, by saving energy and improving the environment. The idea for a strategic business approach is to incorporate the value of social responsibility into the firm's business model. Such an approach will enhance opportunities, increase profits, and expand the firm's market share. In essence, the ultimate goal is not only to contribute in a socially responsible manner to the community but to bring new socially responsible products and services into the marketplace. That degree of social responsibility is the egoistic business model for today's astute business leaders. And the responsibility of such a business leader will be to convince, if necessary, the upper management of the firm, the board of directors, and/or the shareholders that it is in the long-term self-interest of the firm to be perceived, and rightfully so, as a socially responsible and sustainable one.

To illustrate, Unilever, the British-Dutch multinational, has opened a free community laundry in Sal Paulo, Brazil, provides financing to help tomato growing farmers to convert to more environmentally sensitive irrigation systems, and has funded a floating hospital that provides free medical care to people in Bangladesh. In Ghana, Unilever provides safe drinking water to communities; and in India, the company's employees assist women in isolated villages commence small entrepreneurial enterprises. As related by *Business Week*, Unilever CEO, Patrick Cescau, views the company's social responsibility effort as one of its biggest strategic challenges for the 21st century. Cescau explains that since 40% of the company's sales come from consumers in developing countries, assisting these countries to overcome poverty and to safeguard the environment is vital to the company's sustaining its competitive advantage. Cescau's rationale for social responsibility underscores the ethically egoistic justification that "good deeds" will produce strategic and competitive advantages and thus inure to the benefit of the company in the long-term. Another example given by *Business Week* was General Electric, which is taking the lead in developing wind power and hybrid engines. Even Wal-Mart, perennially criticized by labor and human rights groups, was praised for its efforts to save energy and to purchase more electricity derived from renewable sources. GlaxoSmithKline was given credit for investing in poor nations to develop drugs. Moreover, the company was praised for being one of the first major pharmaceutical companies to sell AIDS drugs at cost in 100 countries worldwide. *Business Week* pointed out that such socially responsible behavior by the large pharmaceutical company worked in its favor as the company is working much more effectively with these governments to make sure its patents are protected. In addition, as noted in *Business Week*, the CEO, Jean-Pierre Garner, explained that the company's social responsibility efforts produce other egoistic advantages, such as motivating top scientists to work for the firm, as well as enhancing the overall morale of the company's workforce, which gives the company, stated Garner, a competitive advantage. Another example was Dow Chemical, which is developing and investing in solar power and water treatment technologies. Also, Dow CEO, Andrew N. Liveris, explained that there is a "100% overlap" between the company's business values and its social and environmental values. Toyota was cited as another illustration of a socially responsible firm due to its work with hybrid gas-electric cars. Such practices have given Toyota a very good reputation as a company that makes clean-running and fuel efficient vehicles; and *Business Week*[28] related that this "green" reputation has given Toyota a competitive edge. Another example involves PepsiCo and its charitable-giving program, called Refresh, where Pepsi drinkers can vote online, using votes obtained from the company's products, for "refreshing ideas that change the world"[29]. Winners will have their socially responsible projects funded by the company. Past winners of grants have included cheerleading squads for the disabled students, a project to make school bus windshields more aerodynamic. The Refresh program has been extensively advertised by the company in order to give consumers a "voice" in the company's charitable giving, and also, significantly, to engage consumers, enhance the company's image and brand as a socially responsible one, and in the long-term to increase sales and profits. Business "sustainability" and success emerge as the very practical instrumental reasons given by the companies for their social responsibility efforts. Furthermore, social

---

[28] Engardio, 2007.
[29] Bauerlein, 2011.

responsibility is certainly not just a concept applied in the United States; rather, U.S. Multinational companies doing business overseas as well as foreign companies in their own countries are now actively engaged today in social responsibility activities.

Social responsibility, however, at least to some reasonable degree, may be in the long-term self-interest of business.[30] "Some corporations have long supported social initiatives as a means of enhancing their own profits and long-term viability. Through charitable donations, community programs, or holistic decision-making, corporations have pursued tangible goals, such as improving workforce comfort or engendering customer goodwill, arguing that these actions align with the corporation's ultimate profit-making interests."[31] Significantly, Munch adds that "there is some evidence that these strategies are successful"[32]. Wang and Qian[33] conducted a study of the philanthropic of publicly listed Chinese firms from 2001 to 2006 and found that corporate philanthropy enhances corporate financial performance by enabling firms to elicit better stakeholder responses and to gain political resources. Tyagi[34] reports on studies that support the proposition that corporate social responsibility positively affects "corporate attractiveness." Afsharipour[35], furthermore, reported on an Indian study that revealed a positive relationship between company performance and corporate social responsibility. Maggins and Tsaklanganos[36] report on a series of studies that indicated that "CSR is significant in corporate decision-making because of the relationship between a firm's social policies or

---

[30] CAVICO, MUJTABA, NONET, RIMANOCZY, AND SAMUEL, 2015.
[31] Munch, 2012
[32] Ibid, p. 178.
[33] 2012
[34] 2011, p. 31
[35] 2011.
[36] 2012, p. 663.

actions and its financial performance."

A corporation cannot long remain a viable economic entity in a society that is uneven, unstable, and deteriorating. It makes good business sense for a corporation to devote some of its resources to social betterment projects. To operate efficiently, for example, business needs educated and skilled employees. Education and training, therefore, should be of paramount interest to business leaders. A corporation, for example, can act socially responsible by providing computers to community schools and by releasing employees on company time to furnish the training. AT&T has a formal education program, which it has invested $100 million, whereby high school students "shadow" the company's workers. AT&T employees have volunteered over 270,000 hours of their time for this program[37], and more than one million students have participated in the program. British Petroleum (BP), for example, by marketing itself in Europe and the U.S. as "Beyond Petroleum," before the disastrous Gulf oil spill at least, was regarded as a very socially responsible firm, especially for its environmental and alternative fuel efforts. Another illustration involves the web-search company, Google, Inc., which has committed almost one billion dollars in stock as well as a share of its profits to combat global poverty and to protect the environment[38]. Starbucks Corporation, in addition, has been engaged in a variety of socially responsible activities in Guatemala, such as building health clinics, and also promising to pay its coffee suppliers a premium price if they adhere to certain labor and environmental standards. The Coca-Cola company has teamed with the World Wildlife Fund to protect the arctic habitat by releasing 1.4 billion redesigned white Coke cans each showing a

---

[37] See "Commitment to Communities: People Helping People" at:
http://www.att.com/gen/general?pid=22534
[38] Delaney, 2005.

polar bear, which the company hopes will raise awareness of this cause. Coke made an initial donation of $2 million to the World Wildlife Fund, and Coke will match up to $1 million that Coke drinkers will be able to donate to the campaign. McDonald's is so extensively involved in charitable activities and civic affairs in local communities throughout the United States that it produces through its corporate charitable division, Ronald McDonald House Charities of South Florida, special multi-page advertising supplements to local newspapers to describe the company's many socially responsible activities – from grants, "Wish Lists," scholarships, volunteer work to, of course, the Ronald McDonald House itself.

Business also gains an improved public image by being socially responsible. An enhanced social image should attract more customers and investors and thus provide positive benefits for the firm. Maggins and Tsaklanganos[39] stress social responsibility as part of a "broader concept of success" for an organization, and, accordingly, note that in 2007, around 64% of Fortune 100 companies published a social responsibility report which described their economic, environmental, and social performance. Afsharipour[40] points to evidence from India that indicates that being perceived as a socially responsible firm will result in an enhanced public image and improved customer satisfaction. The organization Business for Social Responsibility conducted a survey in which 76% of consumers stated they would switch to retailers associated with good causes, 76% stated they would switch to brands associated with good causes, and 59% of consumers believed that business should help address community problems[41]. *Business Week[42]* recently provided examples

---

[39] 2012, p. 661.
[40] 2011.
[41] Forman, 1996.
[42] Marketing, 2012.

of companies engaging in socially responsible marketing as one way to persuade consumers to spend in a difficult economy, to wit: Sketchers USA launched a brand called BOBS, meaning Benefiting Others By Shoes, which results in the company donating two pairs of shoes for every one sold; Urban Outfitters features clothes by Threads for Thought, which gives part of its sales proceeds to humanitarian groups; Nordstrom sells hats made by Krochet Kids International, which enlists impoverished people in Uganda and Peru, for example, to make hats which are sold in the U.S. for $24; and Feed Projects, which makes T-shirts, handbags, and accessories, donates a percentage of its profits to United Nations anti-hunger programs. *Business Week*[43] emphasized that when implemented correctly, these socially responsible retailing efforts are good strategies that "do good and make donors feel good too," especially young consumers who may not have the means to make large charitable contributions but who admire brands that are "trendy" but which also reflect a save-the-planet theme. Another example of actively doing social "good" based on a philanthropic definition of "social responsibility" was very nicely "captured" in the title of a *Wall Street Journal* article describing the social responsibility efforts of the Internet search company, Google. The very apt title to the article was "Google: From 'Don't Be Evil' to How to Do Good"[44]. The article related that Google in 2008 announced a major philanthropic venture by which the company will contribute $30 million in grants and investments to a variety of charitable as well as for-profit organizations. Google's civic efforts encompass providing money to predict and prevent diseases, to develop solar power, empower the poor with information regarding public services, and to create jobs by investing in small- and medium-sized businesses throughout the "developing" world in order to boost employment. The essence of the *Wall Street Journal* article was that

---

[43] Ibid, p. 1.
[44] Delaney, 2008.

Google has "graduated" from being a company that "only" refrained from committing harm to a company now actively and substantially engaged in making socially responsible contributions throughout the world, thereby materially enhancing the company's reputation. To further illustrate, the Walt Disney Company, in an effort to portray a socially responsible message, as well as to attract customers to its theme parks, commenced a program, called "Give a Day, Get a Disney Day," whereby the company will give away a million one-day, one-park tickets to people who volunteer at select charities. A corporation that acts more socially responsible not only secures public favor, but also avoids public disfavor. To illustrate, for many years the large multi-national pharmaceutical companies were criticized for not providing AIDS drugs for free or at greatly reduced prices to African governments. In response to public criticism, the pharmaceutical responded in a socially responsible (and also egoistic manner) by giving the drugs away or selling them at cost. Moreover, certain pharmaceutical companies, such as Roche and GlaxoSmithKline, on their social responsibility and sustainability websites have statements indicating preferential pricing and accessibility as well as limited patent policies for AIDs drugs going to African and other less developed countries[45]. Furthermore, these policies have now been extended to states in the United States to provide the drugs to poor patients by means of "Patient Assistance Programs"[46]. Accordingly, social responsibility and also good public relations are achieved. In response to criticism from the Humane Society, the International House of Pancakes (IHOP) now has a social responsibility website that states it is against the cruel treatment of animals, its eggs are "cruelty free," and that the animals used for its food receive "dignified humane treatment." Wal-Mart, the giant retailer, in response to criticisms from environmentalists and labor

---

[45] Roche, 2007; GlaxoSmithKline, 2005.
[46] Tasker, 2011; Tasker, 2010.

activists, now has a director of global ethics, who is responsible for developing and enforcing company standards of conduct, as well as a "senior director for stakeholder engagement," whose role is to develop a new model of business engagement that produces value for society. Similarly, clothing and apparel manufacturers, such as Nike and the Gap, in response to criticism by labor and consumer groups about exploitive working conditions in overseas "sweatshops," have ended abusive working conditions and now report on their social responsibility efforts and achievements overseas. The NBC television network will accept liquor advertisements but, out of a concern of criticism from government regulators and health advocates, only if the advertisements carry a "socially responsible" message, such as urging viewers who drink to have a "designated driver." Exxon-Mobil recently launched a social responsibility campaign to build schools in Angola, which (perhaps not coincidentally) is an emerging oil power. Coca-Cola Co. is very extensively involved in providing clear drinking water to the "developing world," for example, by furnishing water purification systems and lessons to local communities. This meritorious social responsibility effort is designed also to promote "Coke's" reputation as a global diplomat and local benefactor. "Coke," by the way, uses a great deal of water in producing its products.

HR Magazine in a human resources context underscored the egoistic and strategic rationale for a company to be rightly perceived as a socially responsible one. In a constrained and highly competitive global labor market, the shrewd corporate executive will use his or her firm's social responsibility stance to attract new employees, especially top talent, as well as to engage and retain highly skilled and highly motivated current employees. Udgata and Das[47] add that "from

---

[47] 2012, p. 52.

a human resources perspective, the ability to attract top talent is a major challenge for companies. But the best and brightest today are looking for more than impressive salaries and stock prices. They want something more – something that gives meaning to their work and their lives. Supporting social entrepreneurs in different ways shows that companies care about more than the "bottom line." Accordingly, corporate social responsibility can be a key recruitment and retention strategy for the global organization, which business leaders and managers can use to attract, develop, and keep a highly engaged, motivated, and productive workforce.

However, a socially responsible firm must also be a realistic; that is, socially responsible and environmental efforts must be sustainable economically and should have some relationship to the firm's business. Employees should also be engaged directly in the company's social responsibility activities so as to engage them, inspire them, motivate them, and thereby enhance morale and productivity. Moreover, a firm's social responsibility program does not have to be a multi-million dollar effort; rather, something as simple as an employee social responsibility "suggestion box" or as straightforward as a recycling or energy saving program will do to promote employee involvement as well as to promote and give credence to employee social values. Nonetheless, despite the size, a firm's social responsibility efforts should be publicized widely within the company, for example, in company newsletters, as well as externally, for example in company annual "social responsibility" reports. Being socially responsible, therefore, advises *HR Magazine*, is a smart and sustainable business strategy, especially in a human resource context. An actual illustration of *HR Magazine's* social responsibility recommendation is the PepsiCo. The company's chairperson and CEO, Indra Nooyi, has urged companies to follow her company's approach to being a "good" global company; and by "good" she means that in addition to having a strong financial performance, a firm must value and take care of its employees and also the public's health and the environment. For example, PepsiCo has expanded its product lines to include more juices and waters as well as introducing low-sugar versions of its popular "fitness drink," Gatorade. The company is also promoting energy management, for example, by reducing its water usage and creating more environmentally "friendly" packaging. One major benefit of being a socially responsible firm, PepsiCo has discovered, is that its employees are inspired and energized, thereby helping the company to retain employees.

The business leader in guiding his or her firm is now expected to be socially responsible and take a broader stakeholder approach to decision-making. The rationales for doing so are evident. Accordingly, the authors strongly recommend that business leaders take a more sophisticated "strategic" approach to social responsibility. Harish[48] very nicely blends these "strategic" and stakeholder elements to corporate social responsibility:

> Corporate social responsibility (CSR) is a concept whereby organizations consider the interests of society by taking responsibility for the impact of their activities on customer, suppliers, employees, shareholders, communities and other stakeholders, as well as the environment. CSR is a way firms integrate social, environmental and economic concerns into their values, culture, decision-making, strategy and operations in a transparent and accountable manner and thereby establish better practices within the firm, create wealth and improve society. CSR is certainly a strategic approach for firms to anticipate and address issues associated with

---

[48] 2012, p. 521.

their interactions and others and, through those interactions, to succeed in their business endeavors.

So, one and one's business should be socially responsible. That is easily said; yet there are three main social responsibility challenges to the business leader. These challenges are: Who should be in charge of social responsibility? How much social responsibility should one engage in? And what type of social responsibility should one engage in? As to the first, who should be in charge of social responsibility, the authors would recommend a high-level, visible, and empowered ("politically" and financially) position, such as a Vice President of Social Responsibility and/or Sustainability or a Director or Team Leader. Wal-Mart has the position designated as the "Vice-President of Global Corporate Social Responsibility." Yet some companies (in order to ensure good publicity and/or good community relations) have the Director of Marketing or Community Relations in charge of social responsibility and/or sustainability efforts. So long as the position is a "real" one and not mere "window dressing," that is, there is true "substance," then the "form" of the exact title should not be controlling.

Secondly, regarding the extent of social responsibility, the authors would counsel that social responsibility be in the "right" amount, that is, a moderate and prudent amount as befitting the size, stature, and finances of the firm. One does not want to do too much (such as Ben & Jerry's and British Petroleum's Sir John Browne); yet one does not want to do too little (such as "Chainsaw" Al Dunlop and Marie Antoinette of "Let them eat cake" fame – or infamy!). A good example of the "right" amount would be Starbucks Chairman and CEO, Howard Schultz.

The third type of social responsibility challenge for the business leader is what type of social responsibility? The authors thus would recommend actions and activities that are tied to the image, brand, products, and services of the business (which, in essence, is a marketing approach to social responsibility, and thus one that surely will appeal to business people). Some examples might be: the Home Depot and Habitat for Humanity, where the tie-in is obvious; Royal Caribbean building schools and health clinics in Haiti, where it has a major port facility; and Starbucks doing the same in Guatemala, where it buys a great deal of its coffee. To further illustrate, Whole Foods Market has a Green Mission encompassing the following efforts: "green" building standards, a "Reduce, Reuse, and Recycle" program, a pollution awareness campaign, using reusable bags and not plastic bags, rewarding customers who bring their own bags to shop, a charitable donation program of both sales income and food to local charities and environmental groups, sponsoring summer camps, and a program where it makes loans and provides training to local farmers and suppliers. The objective is for people, the community, and the planet to "flourish"[49]. The global professional services firm Ernst & Young, engages in social responsibility and sustainability efforts in the areas of energy conservation and environmental protection, as well as "green" training programs for employees, companies, and home owners, not "merely" to "Build a Better Working World" (which is the title of the firm's Sustainability Report), but also because their employees, job applicants, recruits, clients, and customers "care"[50]. The Hilton Ft. Lauderdale Beach Resort has spearheaded the hotel's chain use of wind energy by means of several (very artistic) roof wind turbines to power in part the hotel. The project cost almost $1 million dollars; and the hotel does not expect to get its "return-on-investment" for several years[51]. Nevertheless, the hotel has acquired a deserved reputation in the

---

[49] Salcedo, 2015.
[50] John, 2015.
[51] Vago, 2015.

community and with tourists from around the world as a socially responsible and sustainable business and thus has obtained some very favorable publicity for its "green efforts." Moreover, in the long-term, the hotel also expects to save money by its "green" efforts (and the authors submit that it is the business leader's responsibility to point out these long-term positive consequences for "going green"). Another example is Carnival Corporation's "social impact travel" cruise where passengers on seven day cruises from Miami can volunteer for socially responsible activities on the ground at the various port stops. In addition to the traditional cruise excursions, passengers can help with local agriculture, work with women's cooperatives, teach English, and help build water filters. Moreover, a portion of the fare will be given to partner organizations on the ground to cover travel, staff, and supplies and to help fund their general operations. These are all obviously beneficial actions to society and ones that demonstrate that a company is a "socially responsible" and "sustainable" one; and the actions will benefit these companies too; and a company should not be shy, the authors believe, in getting some "good PR" to show off their social responsibility and sustainability *bona fides.* And it is not merely the community that will be impressed by a company's "green" efforts. The fact that a company monitors risks, measures its energy and water use, and does not waste energy and water, but rather conserves both, indicates not just to the public but also to business and financial analysts that a company is an efficient and effective one[52].

The authors, therefore, offer the following "socially responsible," as well as self-interested, recommendations to business leaders: For corporations, we recommend that business leaders should increase in a prudent manner the amount of "corporate socially

---

[52] John, 2015.

responsible" activities in order to enhance organizations' "reputational capital." A high corporate reputation of doing "good" can benefit the organization in many ways; it will help organizations attract and retain customers, clients, investors and, of course, talented employees. The employees who work in organizations having the reputation of doing "good" through the corporate social responsibility should exhibit higher level of motivation and commitment to perform better for organizational success. Corporations can also use social responsibility and that concomitant high reputation of doing "good" to help survive any economic downturn. Business leaders through management should involve employees in socially responsible activities, for example, through voluntary activities for community betterment, or "going green" efforts at the workplace, so that they may feel a sense of accomplishment and "belonging" to the organization. Business leaders should also communicate the socially responsible activities done by the organization to the employees in order to achieve higher levels of employee engagement. Finally, business leaders must clearly communicate to top management, to the shareholders, or business owners that social responsibility should not be considered as an expense; rather it should be considered as an investment that provides higher yields in the form of higher customer loyalty, employee engagement, and a good reputation in the community, including the business and financial community. Therefore, business leaders should strategically utilize appropriate resources and proper measures for social responsibility in order to build an elevated reputation for doing "good" in the community and society so as to produce societal benefits and also to achieve the critical, instrumental, and ethically egoistic goal of sustainable organizational success.

Another problem confronting corporate social responsibility, especially in the "constituency" or "sustainability" sense, is resistance from shareholders, who may be more interested in short-term profits than long-term sustainable profits. It is explained that, "today's shareholders – particularly the large institutions that increasingly dominate the stock markets – typically prefer immediate maximization of share value over a more patient approach that is willing to wait for potentially greater returns in the future. This preference leads management to prioritize short-term profits over longer-run considerations. This approach obviously discourages constituency CSR because…benefits to nonshareholders reduce short-term profits and therefore have a negative impact on current share price"[53]. Nonetheless, it is the job of the business leader to educate the shareholders, and perhaps corporate management as well, of the benefits that will accrue to the company and the shareholders by the company acting in a smart, shrewd, and strategic socially responsible manner. Millon[54] emphasizes that "the point is that investment in the well-being of key nonshareholder constituencies – even though costly in the short-run – can generate payoffs in the future that justify these expenditures". Harish[55] agrees, contending that "corporate social responsibility can be of direct economic value. CSR should be treated as an investment, not a cost, much like quality improvement. They can thereby have an inclusive financial, commercial and social approach, leading to a long-term strategy minimizing risks linked to uncertainty." Similarly, and more strongly stated, Spector[56] declares: "posing shareholder and stakeholder interest as an either/or choice is a false dichotomy."

---

[53] Millon, 2011, p. 537.
[54] 2011, p. 539.
[55] 2012, p. 524.
[56] 2012, p. 44.

## D. Conclusion

Business leaders, executives, and managers, as well as applicants for employment, therefore, must be cognizant of and appreciate the instrumental strategic value of social responsibility in its constituency and sustainability formulations. Business leaders, executives, and managers today surely are well aware of societal expectations regarding the social responsibility of their companies. Applicants for positions at these companies should be aware of social responsibility too. Yet applicants must be aware that companies very likely do not want a Ben & Jerry's expansive, but fiscally unrealistic and unsustainable, approach to social responsibility; but rather seek applicants who believe in, can define, and can implement a smart, shrewd, strategic, and ultimately sustainable approach to social responsibility. To illustrate, the recruitment manager for Timberland looks for M.B.A. job applicants "who bring a passion for making the world a better place" and who have a "solid background" in corporate social responsibility, but the company does not want applicants who have "merely" taken academic courses in social responsibility, but students who have "gained practical experience related to social and environmental responsibility." Similarly, the Vice-President of Corporate Social Responsibility and Sustainability for Campbell Soup Company indicated that the company is looking for employees who value social responsibility "as a bottom-line booster, not just something to feel good about." The company, therefore, is looking not just for graduates who have studied the subject of social responsibility, but also those who can understand how to implement corporate social responsibility initiatives so that they can have a real impact and business connection. Accordingly, for job applicants today being socially responsible is a facet of having a good personal business sense as well as doing "good" for a firm and society as a whole.

Business leaders, therefore, must engage in smart, shrewd, and strategic social responsibility. And the rationale for being socially responsible is Ethical Egoism. That is, the instrumental value of being a "socially responsible" person and organization will be the advancement of one's own self-interest, the company's self-interest, as well as the concomitant sustainable benefit to community and society as a whole.

# CHAPTER 6

# Stakeholder Values and Business Leadership

Stakeholder theory was discussed over 40 years ago by Klaus Schwab, the founder and chairman of the World Economic Forum, based in Geneva, Switzerland. Schwab explained that "stakeholder theory…considers the enterprise as a community with a number of stakeholders – in other words, social groups that are directly and indirectly connected to the enterprise and that are dependent on its success and prosperity. These groups include employees, customers, suppliers, the state and especially the society's in which the enterprise is active"[57].

Accordingly, there is today a normative conception of social responsibility; that is, utilizing stakeholder theory to identify philosophical, ethical, and moral guidelines for the operation and management of the corporation. To wit, Hasnas[58] summarizes the fundamental moral implications of stakeholder theory: "Managers of an organization do not have an exclusive fiduciary duty to any one stakeholder group, but rather, are obligated to ensure that the value created by the organization is distributed among all normative shareholders and that all normative stakeholders have input into the managerial decisions that determine how the organization attempts to create that value. Normative stakeholders include the organization's financiers, employees, customers, suppliers, and local communities."

---

[57] Schwab, 2010, p. A19.
[58] 2013, p. 52.

Furthermore, regarding the access criterion, Hasnas[59] adds that "in the traditional stakeholder model of the firm, this implies that managers must either provide a direct avenue of input for or act as a representative of the firm's employees, suppliers, customers, and local communities in deciding how the firm should act." However, for the purposes of this work, we are positing the concept of social responsibility as a value "above and beyond" the law as well as ethics and morality since an organization may neither have a legal duty based on the law nor have a moral duty based on ethics to be a "socially responsible" firm.

In order to illustrate the stakeholders and values involved in business decision-making as well as to show the relationship among stakeholder values, social responsibility, and sustainability, we have prepared a visual table for a quick review. Table 6.1 shows the typical stakeholders in the business realm, that is, those constituent groups who are directly or indirectly affected by corporate actions. The Table then shows what these stakeholders value, that is, what they deem to possess worth - primarily and secondarily. These stakeholder groups typically are the following: shareholders and owners, employees, customers and consumers, suppliers and distributors, creditors, community, government, competition, and society. Shareholders as the "owners" of the corporate entity are always listed first.

---

[59] 2013, p. 55.

Table 6.1 – Stakeholder Values,
Social Responsibility, and Sustainability

| Stakeholders | Primary Values | Secondary Values |
|---|---|---|
| *Owners / Shareholders* | Financial Returns and Income | Growth and Added Value |
| *Employees* | Jobs and Pay | Job Stability and Satisfaction |
| *Customers and Consumers* | Supply of Goods and Services | Quality, Price, and Customer Service |
| *Suppliers / Distributors* | Contract Relationships and Payment | Long-term Relationships |
| *Creditors* | Payment and Rate of Return | Credit-worthiness and Security |
| *Community* | Employment and Tax-base | Philanthropy and Social Responsibility |
| *Government* | Legal Compliance and Tax-base | Competitiveness and Entrepreneurship |
| *Competition* | Market Share | Legal and Ethical Competition |
| *Society* | Growth, Prosperity, Sustainability | Social Responsibility and Environmental Stewardship and Improvement |

*Note*: Table based on "Stakeholders and Their Expectations" by Professor N. Harish (May 2012, p. 522).

Obviously, a corporation cannot survive unless it serves and benefits its shareholders in a financial sense. However, today, shareholders may view their investment as one that benefits other stakeholders and society too. Regardless, all shareholders are entitled to the honest and efficient management of their investment as well as a fair return on their investment. Employees, of course, are interested in obtaining and maintaining employment. They value a just wage, fair employment practices and working conditions, and job security. They also may value working for a company that is regarded as a "socially responsible" one. Customers and consumers want access to goods and services that are of good quality, at a fair price, and that come with good customer service. Suppliers and distributors want financially rewarding, long-term, contractual relationships with the company. Local communities want to see the corporation located in their cities and towns so as to provide employment for the citizens and residents and to support the local tax-base. The local community also values, and very well may expect, that the corporations in its presence participate in civic, charitable, philanthropic, and socially responsible activities. Creditors naturally value being repaid and also expect a fair rate of return as well as adequate assurances of security for the obligation. Government values legal compliance with business laws and business regulations. Government also values business as an important component of its tax-base. Government values, and thus desires to promote, entrepreneurship and competition. As to the competition, the competition values its own market share, yet expects in a capitalistic model "tough" and "hard-hitting" competition, but everyone wants rivalry that is legal and ethical. Society values its survival, of course, and also growth, prosperity for its members, and the sustainability of business and society. Members of society also value today, and thus expect, that the corporation will be a socially responsible one, particularly regarding its stewardship of the environment and other sustainability efforts to improve the environment.

The goal of the business leader today is to balance and harmonize these values; and thus to attempt to devise corporate policies that maximize these values in a legal, moral, socially responsible, and practically efficacious manner, thereby resulting in "win-win" scenarios for the business and all its stakeholders, and thereby attaining a level of continual sustainable business success.

# CHAPTER 7

# Sustainability and the Business Sustainability Continuum

Another important value for business leaders and entrepreneurs to be cognizant of today is "sustainability." Sustainability is an even more expansive variant of "social responsibility." Sustainability is a notion tied to the values of law, ethics, and social responsibility. A basic definition of sustainability is "taking care of people's present needs without compromising future generations." Sustainability, however, is a broad and all-encompassing concept since it can be interpreted as a MEANS (typically in the form of beneficial environmental actions, such as "green" buildings and offices, reducing green-house gasses, and otherwise reducing the firm's "environmental footprint"), and also as an END (that is, having a sustainable organization, society, as well as a sustainable planet for future generations)[60].

Today, the concept of "sustainability" has emerged, along with social responsibility and corporate governance, as important subject matters for business.[61] Paul[62] defines sustainability as follows: "A sustainable business is any organization that participates in environmentally friendly or green activities to ensure that all processes, products, and manufacturing activities adequately address current environmental concerns while maintaining a profit." Being a "green" business, moreover, means that a company is providing

---

[60] Cavico, 2014

[61] CAVICO, MUJTABA, NONET, RIMANOCZY, AND SAMUEL, 2015.

[62] 2012, p. 79

"environmentally friendly" services and products as well as one that has made "an enduring commitment to environmental principles in its business operations"[63]. The term, "The Triple Bottom Line," representing people, planet, and profits, which was created by John Elkington in 1994, also is directly related to sustainability. As explained by Paul[64]: "It is a model or concept for compelling business leaders to consider more than just money. It requires business leaders and owners to balance social, financial, and environmental priorities. The Triple Bottom Line is sustainability – for the business world. The Triple Bottom Line grew out of a realization that we needed to find ways to do business without such a tremendous negative impact on the environment." According to Elkington, the three dimensions of sustainability under the "Triple P" formulation are economic prosperity, environmental quality, and social justice/equity. Sustainability has an ethical component and thus will result in ethical decision-making by companies. Moreover, Gupta[65] asserts that consumers will consider the ethical implications of this decision-making and "will have no qualms about boycotting products and corporations that do not act ethically".

The sustainability approach to corporate social responsibility is premised on the idea that a company must remain economically viable in the long-term; and that in order to be viable the company must take into consideration other stakeholders beyond the shareholders. Millon[66] explains the sustainability approach to corporate social responsibility as simply:

---

[63] Paul, 2012, p. 79.
[64] 2012, p. 81.
[65] 2012, p. 736.
[66] 2011, p. 530-31.

The realization that the corporation's long-run prosperity depends on the well-being of its various stakeholders, including workers, suppliers, and customers. Sustainability also requires ongoing availability of natural resources and a natural environment in which the corporation and its various constituencies can survive and flourish. Well-functioning markets and stable and supportive governments are also essential....The sustainability perspective sees attention to nonshareholders – including investment in their well-being – as essential to the viability and success of the firm and also to the enhancement of shareholder value....Sustainability CSR looks beyond the current quarter or year and factors in long-run benefits as a potential offset to short-term cost.

Porter and Kramer[67] use the term "shared value" to underscore the value of sustainability and for business leaders to use a decision-making criterion in business, to wit: "Policies and operating practices that enhance the competitiveness of a company while simultaneously advancing the economic and social conditions in the communities in which it operates".

However, as Spector[68] correctly points out, dealing with sustainability may be a difficult challenge for certain business executives: "One of the causes may be that the sustainability aim of creating long-term value, while balancing the business need for profit with the ethics of social and environmental responsibility, is uncharged territory for traditional compliance-oriented corporate governance practice." However, Paul[69] provides a similar "instrumental" rationale for sustainability as a "management

---

[67] 2011, p. 66.
[68] 2012, p. 42.
[69] 2012, p. 82.

philosophy," to wit: "For companies, it's no longer good enough to focus only on the financial bottom line. Companies must invest on the social and environmental fronts as well, not only because it's the right thing to do, but for business reasons. Poor performance in the social and environmental areas will ultimately infect financial performance and shareholder value." Sustainability will help the business; but also will help the business help governments solve pressing social problems; and, as such, "this provides an occasion to rebuild trust that is good for business and good for society"[70]. Harish[71] adds that "CSR has been widely regarded as a positive phenomenon helping bridge the gap of social inequality and thus contributing to sustainable development."

Figure 7.1 - The Business Sustainability Continuum (BSC)

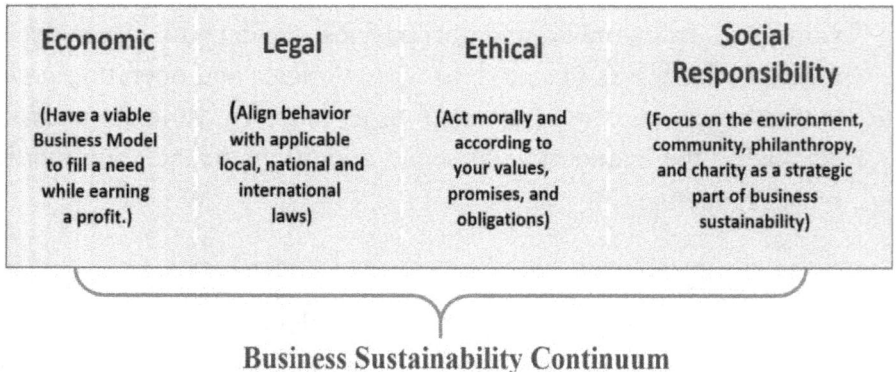

| Economic | Legal | Ethical | Social Responsibility |
|---|---|---|---|
| (Have a viable Business Model to fill a need while earning a profit.) | (Align behavior with applicable local, national and international laws) | (Act morally and according to your values, promises, and obligations) | (Focus on the environment, community, philanthropy, and charity as a strategic part of business sustainability) |

**Business Sustainability Continuum**

In order to better illustrate as well as explicate the values of practical economics, legality, morality, social responsibility, and stakeholder interests, and their relationship to sustainability, we developed a sustainability model, called The Business Sustainability Continuum (BSC); see Figure 7.1. The BSC illustrates that the continual success

---

[70] Spector, 2012, p. 39.
[71] 2012, p. 521.

and "sustainability" of the business can only be achieved by an adherence to four core values: *Economic*, indicating that a business must have a viable business model which fulfills a need and enables the business to make a profit; *Legal*, indicating that this profit must be achieved in legal manner by aligning the conduct of the business with all applicable local, national, and international law; *Ethical*, indicating that since there may be no law or "gaps" in the law, nonetheless the business must act in a moral manner and also must act in conformity with its values, promises, and obligations; and *Social Responsibility*, indicating that the business must focus on the community and engage prudently in civic, philanthropic, and charitable endeavors, as well as environmental conservation and protection efforts, as part of the business' overall strategic sustainability plan.

Accordingly, adherence to these "sustainable" values of economics, legality, morality, and social and environmental responsibility will enable the business to achieve success and to sustain that success in a continual manner, thereby benefiting the business, its shareholders, communities where it does business, and all the stakeholders affected by the business, including society as a whole. Therefore, *as per* the essence of the Business Sustainability Continuum, responsible business leaders, executives, and managers must think strategically and lead themselves, their organizations, communities, society, and the planet toward a sustainable future.

# CHAPTER 8

# The Leadership Mindset

One can debate (and debate continuously) philosophically whether values are "real" intrinsically or merely instrumental; yet it would seem beyond reasonable dispute that the values discussed herein possess instrumental worth to the business leader and the business. Values today increasingly drive consumer and also employee behavior. Consumers will want to do business with, and employees will want to work for, businesses whose values are compatible with their own. Legality, ethics, and morality are very important values; and today social responsibility and sustainability are such values too. Business leaders definitely must be cognizant of these values. Furthermore, the emphasis on stakeholders or constituency groups is an essential component of business leadership. The business leader must take an enlightened approach to satisfying the values of stakeholders in order to achieve long-term sustainable success. As emphasized, the ultimate goal is to attain "win-win" resolutions whereby all the company's stakeholders receive value.

Today, social responsibility, and in the strategic sense the authors have emphasized, emerges as a key element in the business leader achieving stakeholder symmetry and value, business success, and business sustainability. Fundamentally, therefore, business leaders are expected to lead, and to lead by values, encompassing legal values, moral values, and socially responsible values too. Consequently, cognizance of, adherence to, and successfully dealing with the values, not only of legality and morality, but also social responsibility and sustainability, have become imperatives for business leaders.

Modern business leaders, therefore, must recognize that morality and ethics, social responsibility, and sustainability, in addition to the law, are now essential aspects of business. Accordingly, these values must have a prominent place on the business vision, mission, and agenda. The view today is that business should pursue profits (legally and morally, of course), but also that business should also strive to achieve social objectives in a sustainable manner. Business leaders should, and actually are expected to, know and understand the rationales for acting morally as well as for corporate social responsibility and business sustainability. Moreover, business leaders are expected to create and implement corporate strategies to be a legal, moral, socially responsible, and sustainable business.

Many businesses currently are cognizant (or should be) of their moral obligations in addition to their legal duties. Accordingly, many businesses now have Codes of Ethics and thus act, or profess to act, in a moral as well as legal manner. As underscored in this book, today there clearly is a societal expectation that business will truly act morally even in the absence of the law. Moreover, presently, social and environmental responsibility and sustainability are societal expectations too. As a result, social and environmental responsibility as well as sustainability also should be incorporated into business values, missions, and codes. Social responsibility is now an integral part of the modern way, and the sustainable way, to do business.

As the authors also have emphasized throughout this book, social and environmental responsibility also possess instrumental value because it can be used in a smart, shrewd, and strategic sense to help the business achieve and sustain successful performance. Moreover, social responsibility as well as environmental responsibility can, and should, be viewed as business opportunities for the firm. That is, business leaders can create value for the shareholders by taking advantage of business opportunities that arise from the need to solve social and environmental problems. Social responsibility, therefore, is more than mere "pure charity"; rather, in modern business sense, social responsibility is an integral strategic component in a company's endeavor to achieve larger business objectives; and concomitantly, and also propitiously, society as whole is benefitted too by these social and environmental responsibility activities.

Business, therefore, needs, in addition to adherence to legal and moral values, a formal, coherent, transparent, strategic, stakeholder-based, and sustainable policy of social and environmental responsibility. The goal is to make a positive, beneficial, and sustainable contribution to the company's fiscal growth, to overall economic growth, societal growth and development, and to the betterment of the environment and the planet for future generations. So, what is the "mindset" for successful business leadership? The leadership mindset is: legality + morality/ethics + social responsibility + environmental sustainability (means) = sustainable leadership (ends). Accordingly, legality, morality and ethics, social and environmental responsibility, and sustainability are "smart business" and "good business" – for business people, business, and society.

The value of *legality* + the value of *morality/ethics* + the value of *social responsibility* + environmental *sustainability (as a means)* = Sustainable Leadership *(as an ends)*.

---------

# CHAPTER 9

# Summary

The societal expectations today are that business leaders and businesses must act legally, morally, and in a socially and environmentally responsible manner. That is the mindset – the "three value drill" - for business leaders. This mindset is the way to achieve sustainability; and leaders must show the way. Consequently, the challenge for the business leader is to fulfill these expectations and to meet these challenges. The principal objective of focusing on ethics and sustainability at any orientation should be to help current and future leaders to act in conformity with these values and to achieve personal and organizational success. The rationale for adherence to these values (though admittedly not without some cost, effort, and time in the short-run) will be sustainability in the long-term. That is, the leaders will be able to achieve success, and will be able to *sustain* that success for themselves, their families, their companies and organizations, their communities, for society as a whole, all while making their contribution to build a better planet for future generations. The basic "formula," therefore, is: the value of legality + the value of morality/ethics + the value of social responsibility + sustainability (as a means in the form of environmental responsibility) = sustainable leadership (as an end). And such leadership will lead to sustainable business, communities, and society. As Socrates said a long time ago (but which the authors believe is still quite true): "Money comes from virtue." And as the Venetians (the very successful international business people) said in the motto of the old

Venetian Republic, one must act "For the honor *and* profit of Venice". And as the old maxim goes: "One can do well by doing good." So be successful, become prosperous, but be virtuous and honorable; and thus be proud of yourself, make your parents and family proud, make your employers proud, make your community proud, and make your teachers and mentors proud.

The title to this book is "Developing a Legal, Ethical, and Socially Responsible Mindset for Sustainable Leadership." The authors have continually emphasized these three core values to this mindset. The "mindset" is the "three value drill." It is simple and straightforward. In contemplating an action (a sound business one), the business leader must be keenly aware of and ask (because society demands that he or she ask) the three key questions:

1. Is it legal?
2. Is it moral?
3. What should a socially responsible firm do?

Social responsibility, one recalls, includes sustainability as a *means* in the form of environmental actions. And the beneficial result is sustainable leadership as an *ends* in the form of having a sustainable organization, community, society, and planet for future generations by adhering to the three core values. Sustainability, in particular, is emerging as an issue that will dominate the agenda of the business leader for the coming decades. We believe that adherence to these core values are critical to the success, and the sustainable success, of the enterprise. The business leader, therefore, must be cognizant of these issues, and must be prepared to deal, and to deal efficaciously, with them in order to achieve sustainable success.

Success, however, is premised on more than the key values examined and underscored in this book, though they are very important, obviously. As briefly discussed in the beginning of this book, in addition to acting legally, ethically, and in a socially responsible manner, the business leader must in fact be a leader, with all that being a "leader" entails. He or she clearly must set worthwhile and attainable goals; and have the requisite knowledge, skills, expertise to successfully achieve them. The business leader must have the proper "work ethic," manifested by hard-work, diligence, reliability, dependability, and the fulfillment of responsibilities. Moreover, possessing a "pleasant" personality and being a forgiving and compassionate person are also important ingredients for success. Finally, it always helps to have "good luck" in the sense of good fortune too. Yet, the authors firmly believe that you can "make your own luck" by being persistent, persevering, taking advantage of opportunities that come your way, and making your own opportunities. Then you will be successful; and your company, organization, or enterprise will be successful too; and you will be able to sustain that success.

# CASE STUDIES

The following are case studies succinctly presenting business controversies with legal, ethical, and social responsibility ramifications. The authors derived these case studies from current events. The case studies are summaries of articles from journals and periodicals to which the authors have added pertinent laws. The case studies are followed by discussion questions based on the themes and core values explicated in this book, which can be used for analytical debates, group activities, and face-to-face discussion purposes.

## 1. "Made in USA" Products

The *Wall Street Journal* (WSJ) (Aeppel, 2014) reported on a growing controversy involving companies that use the "Made in USA" labels on their products. The problem arises when foreign made components are part of the "USA" products. There are two types of laws that apply to such situations. One is the Federal Trade Commission (FTC) general rule against false, deceptive, and misleading advertising. Specifically, the FTC has a "guideline" regarding products with the "Made in USA" label. The guideline states that the company can use the label on goods but only if "all or virtually all" of the goods are made in the United States. However, the WSJ points out that the FTC does not define the word "virtually." Consequently, the WSJ indicates that companies use a "rule of thumb" that if 70% of more of a good is made in the United States then the goods qualify as American made and the label can be used. But the U.S. is a federal system of government, which means that states may have laws that further restrict the use of the "Made in USA" label. For example, the WSJ points to California, which has the strictest law in the nation. In California, according to the WSJ, even one small foreign component in a large product will preclude a company from saying the product is "Made in USA"; the product must be 100% U.S. made; otherwise, the company can be sued under state consumer law for false advertising. The California law, relates the WSJ, was passed in 1961, and was designed to protect domestic manufacturers from competitors who used cheap foreign goods in their products and who also used the "Made in USA" label. Yet, as the WSJ emphasized, it is increasingly difficult for U.S. manufacturers to avoid using at least some foreign parts in their goods since so much of U.S. manufacturing has now been outsourced overseas.

The WSJ provided some examples of companies in legal difficulties due to these laws. One company is Lifetime Products, Inc., which manufactures basketball hoops in Utah, but the bolts and the net come from China. The products are sold in Sports Authority stores. The company also manufactures a larger basketball system, which also includes German-made shock absorbers. The result has been two consumer suits against the company for false advertising for using the label. The company has defended itself saying that the foreign parts are not available in the United States; and to manufacture them here would be cost prohibitive. The WSJ reported that the two suits were consolidated as a single class action in San Diego in state court, which lawsuit was settled in 2013. The attorneys received $485,000; Lifetime agreed to donate $325,000 to charity; and also to offer discounts to consumers who had purchased basketball equipment in the past. Two named plaintiffs were awarded $4500 and $3500. Lifetime's legal expenses were $535,000. Another lawsuit was against the maker of helium tanks designed for use at parties, which included imported balloons with the tanks. Another example was a California case against Mag Instruments, which produces Maglite Flashlights, because it used small rubber rings and light bulbs from overseas.

Another example is Boston-based New Balance, the sneaker-maker. The company states that only about 70% of the value of its goods made in the U.S. reflect domestic content. For example, the outer soles are imported from China. The company, however, says that it is not misleading consumers because it also informs consumers about the 70% domestic content standard. Some manufacturers have argued that the law in the U.S. should be harmonized at the 70% standard at the federal and state levels. These proposed laws are called "conformity" laws. Some people suggest a label that says "Made in the USA from U.S. and foreign parts." But consumer groups argue for the strict California standard by asserting that if companies want the benefit of the "Made in USA" label they should accept the cost of making all the parts of the product domestically. The FTC is currently studying the matter.

### Bibliography:
* Aeppel, Timothy, "For Factories, Tougher to Say 'Made in USA,'" *The Wall Street Journal*, October 1, 2014, pp. B1, B2.

### Questions for Discussion:
1. Is the current 70% "rule of thumb" practice deceptive? What should the federal "virtually" guideline mean? Should the FTC issue a firm and clear 70% rule, or perhaps a higher percentage? Should any FTC rule preempt the California and other state laws? Why or why not?
2. Is the California law a moral one pursuant to Utilitarian ethics? Why or why not?
3. Is the California law moral pursuant to Kantian ethics? Why or why not?
4. How should an ethically egoistic company approach the use of the "Made in USA" label? Why?
5. What should a socially and environmentally responsible company be doing in the U.S. in the communities where it makes its goods and also in the foreign countries and communities where it purchases its parts? Why?

## 2. Outsourcing Music

The *Sun-Sentinel* newspaper of Ft. Lauderdale, Florida (Verrier, 2014) reported on a developing controversy involving musicians, principally living in Los Angeles, and the big movie studios. In an effort to keep the costs of producing motion pictures down, the studios are now beginning to outsource or offshore music work as opposed to hiring local musicians to work on movies. Music, of course, is a critical component to the artistic, and thus financial, success of any movie.

The *Sun-Sentinel* reported on a labor dispute in 2014 in Los Angeles where a group of local musicians were protesting against Lionsgate, the independent studio that produced the Hunger Games movies. The protesters wore blue and orange T-shirts with the slogan, "Listen Up." The protesters urged Lionsgate to stop sending musicians' jobs overseas and presented a petition to that effect signed by 12,000 people. The rally and protest were sponsored by the American Federation of Musicians (AFM), which had previously organized rallies against Marvel Studios for hiring musicians in London to work on such movies as the Avengers and Iron Man, even though both films were filmed in the United States. The protesters want the studios to stop offshoring and outsourcing music jobs, and, in the words of one musician quoted in the newspaper, to "bring the music home." The protesters are particularly critical of movie studios that have received taxpayer subsidies to film movies in the U.S., but who nonetheless outsource the music work overseas. The protesters cited three Lionsgate examples: Hunger Games, the Twilight Saga: Breaking Dawn, and the Kevin Costner film, Draft Day (about the NFL draft), all of which were filmed in Ohio where the studios received tax benefits, but where the movies were scored in Macedonia.

The *Sun-Sentinel* further reported that this labor unrest comes at a time of "growing anxiety" in the Los Angeles music industry where film work as well as television work has been a major source of income for the hundreds of local professional musician, many of whom use the film work to supplement their income from working in local symphonies, chamber groups, and opera. A large movie can employ more than 100 musicians; and due to that fact, Los Angeles has become a center for some of the world's best musicians. However, more and more film and television production have now moved overseas, and thus local musicians are having a more difficult time in making a living. Presently, the *Sun-Sentinel* indicated that on any given day approximately 2,000 members of the AFM, Local 47, will work on a movie or television show. However, their earnings have decreased in recent years. In 2007, the newspaper reported that union members made $30 in income for music work; but today they earn about $15 million a year. Local 47 represents 7,400 musicians, arrangers, and copyists.

Even if a movie was filmed elsewhere, Los Angeles musicians had counted on the music work for the movie still being done locally, because of the high level of local talent. But today a great deal of that music business has gone to England and especially London, which has always been a draw for composers, due to the rich musical heritage in that country and city. Musicians, especially from orchestras, are now also being utilized in the Czech Republic, Slovakia, and Macedonia by U.S.

movie studios. The offshoring trend has been accelerated by the growth of technology, especially low-cost technology, which has made it easier to open up high-quality recording studios anywhere in the world. Moreover, foreign musicians and orchestras naturally want the work on the movies, as well as the prestige in working on a Hollywood movie, and thus they have been very aggressive in trying to market themselves to the U.S. movie studios. Furthermore, there is growing pressure on the movie studios to save money by hiring lower-cost musicians in Europe, particularly since the studios do not have to pay residuals, and where hourly rates are much lower than in Los Angeles. To illustrate, in Macedonia, a musician might get $10-$15 dollars per hour (and not receive any contributions to health and pension plans), whereas in Los Angeles a musician would get $75 an hour plus benefits. So, the studios are looking for ways to save money, and consequently there has been downward pressure on music fees, and thus the current controversy, related the *Sun-Sentinel*.

*Bibliography*:
- Verrier, Richard, "Making Overtures," *Sun-Sentinel*, May 26, 2014, p. 4D.

*Questions for Discussion:*
1. Do you foresee any legal problems or impediments to the outsourcing of music work by the U.S. film studios? Why or why not? Would a threatened strike by the AFM be effective? Why or why not?
2. Is the outsourcing of music work moral pursuant to Ethical Egoism from the vantage point of the movie studios? Why or why not?
3. Is the outsourcing moral pursuant to the Utilitarian ethical theory? Why or why not?
4. Is it moral pursuant to Kantian ethics? Why or why not?
5. What should a socially responsible movie industry be doing for the Los Angeles community generally and for the musicians specifically?
6. Is it right for a movie studio to accept taxpayer subsidies to film a movie in the U.S., but then outsource and offshore the music component of the movie? Why or why not?
7. For a business to be sustainable over time, does it have to consider the recruitment of talent from anywhere in the world? Why or why not?

## 3. Personality Tests in Employment

The *Wall Street Journal* (WSJ) (Weber and Dwoskin, 2014) reported on a growing controversy in human resource practice and law – the use of personality tests in employment, typically online tests, that are increasingly being used in the hiring process, especially for customer service positions. The WSJ indicated that the tests are being used to not only determine personality traits, but also skills, cognitive abilities, and other characteristics. Moreover, the WSJ indicated that now 60% to 70% of potential employees in the U.S. are being tested, which percentage has increased from 30% to 40% from approximately five years ago. The personality testing business for employment, the WSJ reports, has now grown to a $500 million business; and is growing 10% to 15% a year. The tests are being used more often as well as earlier in the employment process in order to screen applicants for employment. One example provided by the WSJ of a personality test question comes from an online test used by RadioShack for people who apply online for jobs. The question asks: "Over the course of the day, I can experience many mood changes." Another used by Lowe's asks applicants if they "believe others have good intentions." One used by McDonald's states: "If something very bad happens, it takes me some time before I feel happy again." The Kroger supermarket chain has about 80 personality based questions in its basic employment test. For example, job applicants are asked if they "strongly disagree," "disagree," "agree," or "strongly agree" with the following statements: "You are always cheerful" and "You have not big worries."

Employers provide several reasons for the use of personality tests. Xerox Company says that the tests have reduced attrition in high-turnover customer service jobs and in some cases by 20%, the WSJ noted. Xerox explains that it is looking for "compassion" in its pre-employment tests, because job applicants who score high for "empathy" tend to do very well in customer service positions. The tests used by Xerox are provided by a California company called Evolv Inc. A Michigan company called Dial Direct states that the tests allow managers and call-center operators to predict with 30% accuracy which employees will attain the highest performance scores. One representative of a company that provides pre-employment tests contends that the tests can screen out 30% of the applicants who are "least qualified," even before the employer commences to review resumes. Some psychologists assert that the tests have some predictive value. One example as noted in the WSJ would be a test that measures and ranks the applicant's or employee's conscientiousness and work ethic. The WSJ pointed out that some academic studies have shown that there is a connection, but only a small one, between individual personality traits and work performance.

Yet the increased use of personality tests has prompted a debate as to their effectiveness, fairness, as well as legality. Presently, the Equal Employment Opportunity Commission is seeking to determine if personality tests discriminate against people with disabilities. Specifically, as noted in the WSJ, the EEOC s trying to ascertain if the tests preclude people with mental illnesses, such as depression or bipolar disorder, from employment, even if they have the right knowledge and skills for the job. According to the EEOC associate legal counsel, as related by the WSJ, if a job applicant's results on a personality test are affected by the fact that the person has an impairment, and the results are used to preclude the applicant from employment, the employer then must defend the use of the personality test, even if the test was otherwise legal and administered correctly. Consequently, an employer who uses personality tests should be prepared to demonstrate that they are not discriminatory and also that they do not have an adverse or disparate (that is, disproportionate) impact on job applicants and employees based on the race, gender, national origin, and disability status.

The WSJ also noted that there is some state law on point. For example, in 2011, Rhode Island government regulators ruled that there was probable cause to conclude that the CVS drugstore chain violated a state law prohibiting employers from eliciting information about the mental health or physical disabilities of job applicants. The company's personality test asked job applicants if they agreed or disagreed with the following statements: "People do a lot of things that make you angry." "There's no use in having close friends; they always let you down." Many people cannot be trusted." And "You are unsure of what to say when you meet someone." CVS removed the questions and settled the civil case of discrimination, which was filed by the Rhode Island American Civil Liberties Union, but CVS neither admitted nor denied any wrongdoing. One point is clear, however, and that is the use of such personality tests will increase, and so will the legal, ethical, and practical debate.

### *Bibliography:*

* Weber, Lauren and Dwoskin, Elizabeth "As Personality Tests Multiply, Employers Are Split," *The Wall Street Journal*, September 30, 2014, pp. A1, A12.

### *Questions for Discussion:*
1. Discuss the legal issues involved in this controversy, especially under the Americans with Disabilities Act. How should these issues be resolved?
2. Is it moral for a company to use personality tests pursuant to Utilitarian ethics? Why or why not?
3. Is it moral for a company to use personality tests pursuant to Kantian ethics? Why or why not?
4. How should an ethically egoistic company approach the issue of personality tests? Why?
5. What should a socially responsible company be doing in the community for people with mental health issues? Why?

## 4. Employer Wellness Programs

The *Wall Street Journal* (Weber, 2014) reported on an important development regarding the legality of employer wellness programs, which are programs designed to improve employee health (and also reduce employer health care costs). These programs have expanded greatly in recent years; and now many employers have some type of wellness program (Cavico, *et. al.*, 2014). However, their continued use has been called into question recently because the Equal Employment Opportunity Commission (EEOC) is bringing legal actions in federal court against two companies, arguing that their wellness programs violate the Americans with Disabilities Act of 1990 (ADA).

Wellness programs are divided into two types, colloquially called "carrots" and "sticks." In the former approach, employers reward employees for their participation in wellness programs with discounts on their insurance premiums or additional money in their reimbursement accounts; whereas in the "sticks" approach penalize employees who do not take advantage of the wellness program or do not meet certain "wellness" requirements by adding a surcharge to insurance premiums (Cavico, *et. al.*, 2014; Weber, 2014). The Affordable Care Act (aka "Obama Care") actually encouraged the growth of both types of wellness programs by increasing the incentives as well as penalties that employers could use (Cavico, *et. al.*, 2014; Weber, 2014). The *Wall Street Journal* (Weber, 2014, p. B8) reported on a study by the National Business Group on Health that 74% of employers with wellness programs plant to offer incentives in 2014 compared to 57% in 2009. The EEOC reported on a study by the Kaiser Family Foundation that 94% of employers with over 200 employees, as well as 63% of smaller employers, offer some type of wellness program (EEOC, Press Release, 5-8-13).

The *Wall Street Journal* (Weber, 2014) provided some examples of "penalties," to wit: In Maryland, the state as part of its insurance coverage for employees can impose penalties as much as $450 per person by 2017 for those employees who fail to undergo certain medical screenings and fail to comply with treatment plans for chronic conditions. The wellness program could save the state as much as $4 billion over the next decade, the *Wall Street Journal* reported (Weber, 2014). Another "sticks" example was CVS Health Corp., where employees who do not complete an annual health risk assessment and health screening will pay $600 a year more for their insurance premiums. An example of the "carrots" approach provided by the *Wall Street Journal* (Weber, 2014) is JetBlue Airways Corp., which places as much as $400 a year into full-time employees' health savings or reimbursement accounts for participating in about 45 designated activities, such as attending a smoking-cessation program or completing an "Ironman" race. Moreover, the company is planning on another wellness program that provides employees with as much as $500 based on their body-mass index. Yet employers now must be concerned that their well-intentioned (as well as self-interested-intentioned) wellness program will engender lawsuits.

Wellness programs are governed by many laws (Cavico, *et. al.* 2014). Accordingly, they must be created and implemented in a manner that is in conformity with federal equal employment and anti-discrimination law, particularly the Americans with Disabilities Act. The ADA does not prohibit employer wellness programs for employees. Moreover, as part of a wellness program, which, it must be emphasized, is voluntary, the ADA permits voluntary medical examinations, histories, and inquiries, including disability-related questions, which are part of the wellness program, and without the employer having to demonstrate that they are job-related and consistent with business necessity (EEOC, *Enforcement Guidance*, 2000; EEOC, Office of the Legal Counsel, Informal Discussion Letter, 2011). These programs can encompass, suggests the EEOC, blood pressure screening, cholesterol testing, glaucoma testing, and cancer detection screening (EEOC, *Enforcement*

*Guidance*, 2000). However, any medical records and information obtained as a result of the wellness program must be kept confidential and maintained separately from personnel records; moreover, the records cannot be used to limit health insurance eligibility or prevent occupational advancement (EEOC, *Enforcement Guidance*, 2000). The EEOC will deem a wellness program to be "voluntary" so long as the employer does not require participation and does not penalize employees who do not participate (EEOC, *Enforcement Guidance*, 2000; EEOC, Office of the Legal Counsel, Informal Discussion Letter, 2011).

Significantly, in 2014, the EEOC instituted two lawsuits against companies contending that their wellness programs violate the Americans with Disabilities. The ADA makes it illegal for employers to discriminate against employees and job applicants based on their physical and mental disabilities. The law also requires employers to provide reasonable accommodations to employees and job applicants who need such accommodations because of their disabilities, unless so doing would impose an undue burden or hardship on the operation of the employer's business (Americans with Disabilities Act of 1990). The first EEOC lawsuit, filed in federal court in August of 2014, was against a Wisconsin company, Flambeau, Inc. The second was filed in October of the same year against another Wisconsin company, Orion Energy Systems. In the *Flambeau* case (*EEOC v. Flambeau, Inc.*, 2014), the EEOC contends that Orion violated the ADA by requiring an employee to submit to medical exams and inquiries that were not job related and consistent with business necessity as part of the company's wellness program, which was *not* voluntary. Moreover, the EEOC contends that the company retaliated against the employee in violation of federal law when she complained about the wellness program. In the *Orion* case (*EEOC v. Orion Energy Systems*, 2014), the EEOC contends that Orion violated the ADA by requiring an employee to submit to medical testing and an assessment in connection with the company's wellness program or face what the EEOC deemed to be "dire consequences" (EEOC, *Press Release*, 10-1-14, EEOC Lawsuit Challenges Flambeau Over Wellness Program). Specifically, the company's wellness program required employees to submit to biometric testing as well as a "health risk assessment," or face cancellation of their medical insurance, unspecified "disciplinary action" for the failure to attend the testing, as well as a requirement that the employee pay the full premium price in order to remain covered by the insurance plan; whereas employees who participated were only required to pay 25% of their premium cost. The EEOC deemed these consequences to be "severe" (EEOC, *Press Release*, 10-1-14, EEOC Lawsuit Challenges Flambeau Over Wellness Program).

A key issue for the EEOC will be just how voluntary a "voluntary" wellness program is. As such, a quote from John Hendrickson, the regional attorney for the EEOC in Chicago, is instructive, to wit:

> Employers certainly may have voluntary wellness programs – there is no dispute about that – and many see such developments as a positive development....But they actually have to be voluntary. They can't

compel participation by imposing enormous penalties such as shifting 100 percent of the premium cost for health benefits onto the back of the employee or just firing the employee who chooses not to participate. Having to choose between responding to medical exams and inquiries – which are not job-related – in a wellness program, on the one hand, or being, on the other hand, is no choice at all" (EEOC, Press Release, 8-20-14, EEOC Lawsuit Challenges Orion Energy Wellness Program and Related Firing of Employee).

Another key issue the existence of alternatives in a wellness plan for those employees who cannot participate or meet the standards thus cannot receive the benefits or must pay the penalties There are also other important related issues – legal and ethical – of privacy and compulsion. That is, regarding compulsion, just how coercive can a wellness program be, even if it ultimately benefits the employee. The *Wall Street Journal* (Meyer, 2014, p. B8) reported on a recent workplace survey. In the survey, a poll by the Kaiser Family Foundation indicated that 62% of respondents stated it was not appropriate for employers to require employees to pay more for their health insurance premiums if they do not participate in wellness programs.

Based on the EEOC's interpretation of the ADA in the context of wellness programs, certain basic points are clear:

- Disability-related inquiries and medical examinations are allowed by employers as part of a *voluntary* wellness program.
- A wellness program will be deemed "voluntary" only if the employer neither requires participation *nor penalizes* employees who do not participate.
- Assuming a program is voluntary, and the program requires employees who participate to meet certain health standards or outcomes or to engage in or refrain from certain activities, the employer nevertheless must provide a reasonable accommodation (assuming no undue burden or hardship) to those employees who are unable to meet the requirements of the wellness program due to a disability (EEOC, Office of the Legal Counsel, Informal Discussion Letter, 2013).

The key questions that have not yet been answered by the EEOC and the courts, and which certainly "cry" for clarification, are twofold: Whether and to what extent a reward will amount to a requirement to participate, thus rendering the wellness program involuntary? And whether withholding an award from non-participants will be construed as a penalty, again rendering the program involuntary, and thus illegal? Hopefully, and presumably, the EEOC litigation against the Orion and Flambeau companies and the resulting federal district court decisions will produce some clear standards. Until then, employers should be very carefully that their wellness programs, though well-intended, are construed as involuntary because of the nature of the financial penalties for employees who do not participate or who are denied financial rewards for choosing not to participate. Furthermore, employers must be careful not to penalize people with disabilities because they are not sufficiently "well" to participate or meet wellness standards. Consequently, the authors would advise employers to proceed with extreme caution in adopting wellness plans, and thus to take heed of the old adage, "No good deed goes unpunished."

### Questions for Discussion:
1. Discuss the legal issues involved with wellness programs and the ADA? How should the courts rule on the EEOC lawsuits? Why? What standards should the EEOC promulgate regarding the level of rewards and penalties for wellness programs?
2. Are wellness programs with a penalty moral pursuant to Utilitarian ethics? Why or why not?
3. Are they moral pursuant to Kantian ethics? Why or why not?
4. How should an Ethically Egoistic employer approach wellness programs considering the EEOC litigation? Why?
5. What should a socially responsible employer be doing regarding the health of its employees as well as for people in the community?

### *Bibliography*:
- Americans with Disabilities Act of 1990, 42 *United States Code* Sections 12101-12117.
- Cavico, F.J., Mujtaba, B. G., Muffler, S.C., and Samuel, M. (2014). Wellness Programs in the Workplace: An Unfolding Legal Quandary for Employers. *International Journal of Occupational Health and Public Health Nursing,* Vol. 1, No. 1, pp. 15-50.
- *EEOC v. Flambeau, Inc.*, Civil Action No. 3:13-cv-00638 (U.S. District Court for the Western District of Wisconsin 2014).
- *EEOC v. Orion Energy Systems*, Civil Action No. 1:14-cv-010119 (US. District Court for the Eastern District of Wisconsin 2014).
- Equal Employment Opportunity Commission (July 27, 2000). *Enforcement Guidance: Disability-Related Inquiries and Medical Examinations of Employees Under the Americans with Disabilities Act* (ADA). Retrieved October 9, 2014 from: http://www.eeoc.gov/policy/docs/guidance-inquiries.html.
- Equal Employment Opportunity Commission (June 24, 2011). Office of the Legal Counsel. *Informal Discussion Letter*. ADA and GINA: Incentives for Workplace Wellness Programs. Retrieved October 9, 2014 from: http://www.eeoc/gov/foia/letters/2013/ada_wellness_programs.html.
- Equal Employment Opportunity Commission (January 18, 2013). Office of the Legal Counsel. *Informal Discussion Letter*. ADA: Voluntary Wellness Programs & Reasonable Accommodation Obligations. Retrieved October 9,

2014 from:
http://www.eeoc/gov/foia/letters/2013/ada_wellness_programs.html.

- Equal Employment Opportunity Commission, *Press Release* (5-8-13). Employer Wellness Programs Need Guidance to Avoid Discrimination. Retrieved October 9, 2014 from:
http://www1eeoc.gov//eeoc/newsroom/release/5-8-13.cfm.

- Equal Employment Opportunity Commission, *Press Release* (8-20-14), EEOC Lawsuit Challenges Orion Energy Wellness Program and Related Firing of Employee. Retrieved October 9, 2014 from:
http://www1.eeoc.gov//eeoc/newsroom/release/8-20-14.cfm.

- Equal Employment Opportunity Commission, *Press Release* (8-20-14), EEOC Lawsuit Challenges Flambeau Over Wellness Program. Retrieved October 9, 2014 from: http://www1.eeoc.gov//eeoc/newsroom/release/10-1-14b.cfm.

- Equal Employment Opportunity Commission. *What You Should Know about the EEOC and Enforcement of the Americans with Disabilities Act.* Retrieved October 9, 2014 from:
http://www1.eeoc.gove//eeoc/newsroom/wysk/ada_enforcement.cfm.

- Weber, Lauren, "A Health Check for Wellness Programs," *The Wall Street Journal*, October 8, 2014, pp. B1, B8.

## 5.  SEC Pay Ratio Rule

The *Wall Street Journal* (WSJ) (Lublin, 2014) reported that the U.S. Securities and Exchange Commission will propose a rule (also called a "regulation") that will legally compel companies to disclose how much more the company CEO makes compared to the average employee. Pursuant to the rule, the SEC will require in company proxy-statement disclosures for 2016 that companies ascertain the pay rate for their median worker and compare that amount with the CEO's pay.

The WSJ emphasized that "at a time when pay disparities are a hot political and business issue, the coming rule may put businesses in the sticky spot of having to explain why the highest executive is rewarded so richly while regular workers make comparatively little" (Lublin, 2014, p. B9). The WSJ reported that "total direct compensation for CEOs at public companies increased 5.5% to a median of $11.4 million in 2013" (Lublin, 2014, p. B9). The WSJ also reported on a study by the labor organization, the AFL-CIO, which indicated that CEO pay across a broad sample of 500 companies disclosed that the average CEO earned 331 times more than the typical U.S. worker in 2013; and that in 1980 that ratio was 42 times (Lublin, 2014, p. B9).

Some of the adverse consequences for business of the proposed rule could be negative reactions from media, consumer and labor groups, and shareholders and investors, as well as morale problems among employees if there is a large disparity in the pay ratio (Lublin, 2014). The WSJ reported that "critics say such pay ratios matter little to investors and could make executives easy targets for populist anger or hostile shareholders" (Lublin, 2014, p. B9). Furthermore, the WSJ indicated that "significant differences in pay can affect morale, product quality and turnover, studies have found. Pay-ratio revelations could cause fresh management problems once individuals realize they make less money than their employer's median worker" (Lublin, 2014, p. B9). Employees very well could ask why they are being paid less than the median, let alone much less than the CEO!

The WSJ also reported on a controversy involving Wells Fargo CEO, John Strumpf, whose total 2013 compensation was $19.3 million compared to a company data processing employee who made $15 an hour and who sent a message of the wage comparison to the company's 200,000 employees (Lublin, 2014). The employee also said that the company's lower-level employees "are grossly underpaid for the amount of profit we drive" and that the CEO "should be looking out for his employees when people are struggling to make ends meet" (Lublin, 2014, p. B9). However, supporters of the SEC rule state that they hope that the disclosure will cause companies to reduce corporate leaders' compensation packages as well as to raise the pay of employees, especially lower-level employees (Lublin, 2014).

One problem with enforcing the rule is to determine who exactly is the median, average, or typical employee for comparison purposes, especially for a large company with a diverse, dispersed, and global workforce? In particular, the WSJ stated that "businesses with numerous lower-paid employees abroad will likely report higher ratios than domestic-focused ones" (Lublin, 2014, p. B9). Another problem is that the SEC proposed rule includes part-time and temporary employees, which obviously would inflate the ratio. Yet the SEC is not clear on how companies should determine who their median worker is. Accordingly, companies may compare their CEO's compensation to that of their median, full-time, U.S. worker.

### *Bibliography:*

- Lublin, Joann S., "The Boss Makes How Much More Than You"? *The Wall Street Journal*, November 26, 2014, p. B9.

### *Questions for Discussion:*
1. Should such a pay ratio law be promulgated by the SEC, an administrative agency, or by a statute from the U.S. Congress? Why?
2. How should an Ethically Egoistic company decide who its median worker is as well as how to mitigate any negative consequences from publicizing the ratio?
3. Is the proposed rule moral pursuant to Utilitarianism? Why or why not?
4. Is it moral pursuant to Kantian ethics? Why or why not?
5. Do you agree with the comments of the Wells Fargo employee? Why or why not?
6. What should a very well compensated CEO be doing to be a socially responsible one?
7. What should such a CEO be doing to be a sustainable leader?

## 6.  J.P. Morgan Bank in China

This case study examines J.P. Morgan Chase & Company (J.P. Morgan) and its employment recruitment practices in China (that is, the People's Republic of China, including Hong Kong). The bank's hiring practices are currently being investigated by the U.S. government to determine if the bank violated the U.S. Foreign Corrupt Practices Act (FCPA). The U.S Department of Justice and the Securities and Exchange Commission are seeking to determine if the bank hired the relatives of high-level state officials in charge of large state enterprises in order to secure business from state companies in China. In essence, the U.S. government is trying to ascertain if J.P. Morgan committed an illegal bribe in violation of the FCPA. In 2013, the *Wall Street Journal* (Palazzolo, Matthews, and Ng, 2013), the *New York Times* (Protess and Silver-Greenberg, 2013), and the *Miami Herald* (Protess, Ben and Silver-Greenberg, 2013;Silver-Greenberg, Protess, and Barboza, 2013) reported that J.P. Morgan is being investigated by the U.S. government for allegedly bribing Chinese government officials in violation of the Foreign Corrupt Practices Act (FCPA). Both the Department of Justice and the Securities and Exchange Commission (SEC) have opened bribery investigations to determine whether the bank's practice of giving jobs to the children of high-level, powerful government officials in order to help the bank obtain lucrative business deals with the Chinese government and/or entities dominated or controlled by the government. The *New York Times* (Protess and Silver-Greenberg, 2013) reported that recruitment effort, called the "Sons and Daughters" program, initially arose around 2006 and seemingly peaked around 2009. The bank had been losing several large business deals to competitors who were engaging in hiring of relatives of officials of state enterprises in China; and the "Sons and Daughter's" program was the bank's response. At the time the China economy was "booming" and state enterprises were using banks to raise billions of dollars in stock and debt offerings; but, according to the *New York Times* (Protess and Silver-Greenberg, 2013, p. 1), "J.P. Morgan was falling further behind in capturing that business."

In one recruitment example, J.P. Morgan hired the son of a former Chinese banking regulator who is now the chairman of the China Everbright Group, which is a state-controlled financial conglomerate. Once the chairman's son was hired, the bank secured several contracts from the Chinese conglomerate (Palazzolo, Matthews, and Ng, 2013; Protess, Ben and Silver-Greenberg, 2013; Silver-Greenberg, Protess, and Barboza, 2013). To further illustrate, the Hong Kong office of J.P. Morgan also hired the daughter of a Chinese railway official. The official is also being investigated by the Chinese government for purportedly awarding government contracts in exchange for cash bribes. The China Railway Group is a state-controlled construction company that builds railways for the Chinese government. The Railway Group was in the process of selecting J.P. Morgan to advise it on plans to become a public company (Palazzolo, Matthews, and Ng, 2013; Protess, Ben and Silver-Greenberg, 2013; Silver-Greenberg, Protess, and Barboza). The typical "Sons and Daughters" job paid between $70,000 to $100,000 a year (Protess and Silver-Greenberg, 2013). The *New York Times* (Protess and Silver-

Greenberg, 2013) reported that the "Sons and Daughters" program apparently had some success, as in 2009 J.P. Morgan was 13th among banks in obtaining business in China; but by 2013 the bank had risen to 3rd in market share in China. Accordingly, a key question emerges as to whether there is a sufficient and demonstrable causal link and connection between J.P. Morgan's recruitment practices in China and its growth in business in that country. Did the bank wrongfully direct business to itself by means of the hiring? Specifically, are the bank's recruitment practices illegal bribes in violation of the Foreign Corrupt Practices Act or merely "good" business networking practices?

The U.S. government is investigating J.P. Morgan, as it has and is doing to other companies, to determine if the bank violated the Foreign Corrupt Practices Act, which makes the payment of a bribe, either in the form of money or "anything of value," to a foreign government official, a serious crime as well as a civil wrong (Cavico and Mujtaba, 2014; Cavico and Mujtaba, 2011). Typically, the Justice Department brings criminal prosecutions for violation of the law; and the Securities and Exchange Commission proceeds against wrongdoers civilly. The government is very concerned that U.S. companies are not only hiring the children and relatives of Chinese government officials, but that the U.S. companies are hiring them for "no show" or fake jobs as an indirect way of concealing the transfer of illegal cash payments to the government officials (Palazzolo, Matthews, and Ng, 2013; Protess, Ben and Silver-Greenberg; Silver-Greenberg, Protess, and Barboza). That is, the government is investigating to determine if the hiring of relatives amounts to an illegal bribe pursuant to the FCPA. Neither the U.S. investigation, so far, nor Chinese government documents and public records, definitely link J.P. Morgan's hiring practices to its ability to secure business. Moreover, there is no evidence to date that any of the employees hired were unqualified or that the jobs were fake ones. Nor is there any evidence yet that the employees themselves helped J.P. Morgan obtain business (Palazzolo, Matthews, and Ng, 2013; Protess, Ben and Silver-Greenberg, 2013; Silver-Greenberg, Protess, and Barboza). Nonetheless, U.S. investigators suspect that the bank routinely hired young associates who came from well-connected Chinese families whose members ultimately offered JPMorgan state consulting and other business for the hiring (Palazzolo, Matthews, and Ng, 2013; Protess, Ben and Silver-Greenberg, 2013; Silver-Greenberg, Protess, and Barboza).

The first legal point to address is whether the officials allegedly being bribed by J.P. Morgan are in fact "foreign government officials," as the statute requires. However, as Chow, Daniel (2012, pp. 1022-25) points out, the U.S. government takes an expansive view pursuant to the FCPA as to who in the host country qualifies as a government official. Accordingly, if a Chinese company involved in the J.P. Morgan bribery allegations is state-owned, wholly or partially, state-dominated, state-controlled, or state-subsidized, the officials therein, who are typically high-level ones with discretionary power over contracts and business, would be deemed to be foreign government officials (Chow, Daniel, 2012, pp. 1022-25). As Chow, Daniel (2012, p. 1025) warns: "These expansive definitions of state-owned and state-controlled enterprises as instrumentalities of the state and employees of such entities as foreign officials create significant risks for companies under the FCPA."

The second legal point to address is whether the hiring is in fact an illegal bribe pursuant to the FCPA. The statute does not specifically use the word "bribe" but rather can deem a criminal and civil wrong based on the transfer of "anything of value" to the foreign government official (Cavico and Mujtaba, 2014; Cavico and Mujtaba, 2011). That key term, "anything of value," under the FCPA has been very broadly construed by the Department of Justice and the SEC. Chow (May 2014, pp. 1186-87) emphasizes that the "giving of 'anything of value' to a foreign official in order to obtain or retain business does not have to be in cash. The DOJ has interpreted the term 'anything of value' in an expansive manner." Thus the hiring one's relatives should suffice as a transfer of something of value, though indirect (Cavico and Mujtaba, 2011). Actually, even an offer of employment should be adequate to satisfy the "value" requirement (Cavico and Mujtaba, 2011). The term "foreign officials" is also broadly defined by the FCPA; as such, any person who receives at least a part of his or her salary from the public treasury of a foreign government is considered to be a foreign government official (Cavico and Mujtaba, 2011). Consequently, the Chinese officials in the J.P. Morgan case, as high-level employees of state-owned or -dominated companies, would certainly be construed as foreign government officials for FCPA purposes.

However, in order to demonstrate a violation of the FCPA the government must also prove that the entity that paid the money or transferred something of value, directly or indirectly, to the foreign government official did so with a "bad" or corrupt intent; that is, the intent was to wrongfully direct business to one's company or firm by inducing a person, a Chinese government official in the case herein, to misuse his or her official position to grant the contract or business to the bank, which perhaps based on objective standards it did not deserve (Cavico and Mujtaba, 2011). Under the old English common law, this requisite bad or corrupt intent, the classic "evil mind," was called "scienter" (Cavico and Mujtaba, 2014; Cavico and Mujtaba, 2011). The essence of the "corrupt" intent is to obtain some type of unearned and undeserved preference or to otherwise accomplish some other unlawful result. However, there is no legal requirement that the transfer of "value" violate the law of the host country (Cavico and Mujtaba, 2011). Yet proving such "corrupt" intent is very difficult for the government to do, especially in a criminal case where the evidentary standard is "proof beyond a reasonable doubt" (as opposed to a "preponderance of the evidence" standard for a civil case) (Cavico and Mujtaba, 2014). Evidence, of course, can be direct in the form of witnesses and documents or indirect or circumstantial (Cavico and Mujtaba, 2014). For example, the closer the hiring was to the obtaining of the contract or benefit, the easier it will be for the government to show an improper nexus or connection, at least by circumstantial evidence. Similarly, the closer the relationship between the recipient of a company's largess and the foreign government official the more a jury can infer corrupt intent. To further illustrate in the case herein, even if the bank's hiring of the children of a government official was motivated by a desire to create "good will," to "network," and to curry favor with the foreign official, that mind-set does not necessarily mean that the hiring is corrupt and a bribery crime has been committed, assuming that otherwise the hiring was appropriate. Actually, as reported by the *Wall Street Journal* (Glazer, Fitzpatrick, and Eaglesham, 2014, p. C1), J.P. Morgan Chairman and Chief Executive, James Dimon, stated in a January 2014 interview on CNBC that "it has been a 'norm for years' for banks to hire 'sons and daughters of companies' and to give them 'proper jobs' without violating the law." The bank has long insisted that its program is a lawful one (Protess and Silver-Greenberg, 2013). Consequently, the government is looking for some type of documents or witnesses that would show or testify to a *quid-pro-quo*, that is, a causal connection or link between the hiring and the business opportunities. Was the business obtained wrongfully as a result of the hiring of the relatives, and thus was the requisite corrupt intent was present (Curran and Eaglesham, 2014)? Those are key legal issues. As Chow (2014, p. 1187) explains: "Asking for favors, such as helping a child or relative, is a common practice in China and most people in China not only accept the practice but see nothing wrong with the practice. However, such a practice could trigger liability under the FCPA, especially where there is a *quid pro quo*, i.e., the obtaining of business in return for a non-monetary favor given to a Chinese official." From an evidentiary standpoint, what might be damaging to the bank might be a series of emails reported by the *Wall Street Journal* (Levin, Glazer, and Matthews, 2015, p. A1) that the bank hired the son of the Chinese Commerce Minister despite the fact that his son did poorly on his job interview, did not competently handle his work visa process, sent a sexually inappropriate email to a human resource officer, and was described as "immature, irresponsible, and unreliable." Furthermore, the *Wall Street Journal* (Levin, Glazer, and Matthews, 2015, p. A1) indicated that the Commerce Minister said he would "go extra miles for the bank" if the bank hired his son.

Another fact that might bolster the government's evidentiary case is that the bank apparently was warned in 2011 that there might be some problems with its "Sons and Daughters" hiring program in China as well as Asia. The *Wall Street Journal* (Glazer, Fitzpatrick, and Eaglesham, 2014, p. C1) reported that in 2011 a bank official in Asia alerted bank legal and compliance officers in New York regarding anonymous accusations that the local bank officials recruited either a "prominent" son or daughter of a "senior Chinese official" in order to help the bank obtain and investment-banking contract. J.P. Morgan officials "later discussed those accusations" but "dismissed them"; yet nonetheless the bank's board of directors approved additional anti-corruption measures, including proposing changes to hiring practices in Asia (Glazer, Fitzpatrick, and Eaglesham, 2014, p. C1). What also might assist the government in securing evidence is the "whistleblowing" provision in the Dodd-Frank financial reform law of 2010 which grants employees (as well as other individuals including company "outsiders") who undercover and disclose fraud and other illegality, including violations of the FCPA, to government regulators. These whistleblowers can get a reward of 10-30% of the monetary penalties collected by the government (Jones and Lublin, 2010; Holzer and Johnson,

2010). Another legal requirement as per the FCPA that likely could arise in the J.P. Morgan situation is the "knowing" requirement. That is, pursuant to the statute, there must be evidence that the transfer of value occurred by a party "knowing" that it was given directly or indirectly to the foreign government official (Cavico and Mujtaba, 2011). The objective of this "knowing" requirement is to prevent companies from claiming ignorance of improper payments by their employees, agents, independent contractors, and subsidiaries to foreign government officials; that is, to prevent companies from using the "ostrich" (the "head-in-the-sands" approach) to avoid culpability. Of course, if a company actually knew of the improper payments or authorized or directed them to the foreign government officials there will be legal liability (Cavico and Mujtaba, 2011). Moreover, if a company acted in reckless disregard of the facts, or in conscious indifference thereto, or was aware of a high probability or substantial likelihood of illegal payments, then the "knowing" requirements will be satisfied (Cavico and Mujtaba, 2011). As Gorman (2014, p. 1194) warns: "Indeed, the company can quickly find itself in the middle of a DOJ or SEC FCPA investigation tied to the actions of local agents and affiliates."

In the J.P. Morgan situation herein, as mentioned, the fact that the company might have been warned by its personnel in Asia that its hiring practices, perhaps some of which were inappropriate, occurred would surely be evidence that the bank met the "knowing" requirement regarding the purportedly illegal payments. To further substantiate the "knowing" requirement is evidence that the bank in fact had apparently created the program at a high-level and had a name for the program that clearly indicated its intent; the recruitment effort, as noted, was called the "Sons and Daughters" program (Gorman, 2014, p. 1207). The very name of the recruitment program indicates that higher level bank executives at headquarters not only knew about the program but perhaps created it, authorized it, and directed the program. Moreover, the *New York Times* (Protess and Silver-Greenberg, 2013) reported that bank executives tracked how their hires of well-connected employees led to business with Chinese government entities. So, it appears that it will be difficult for the bank to attenuate the "chain of causation" and to say defensively it was "merely" its "bad" local personnel in China engaging in any wrongdoing.

### *Questions for Discussion:*
1. Is J.P. Morgan bank acting legally in China? Why or why not?
2. Is the bank acting morally pursuant to Ethical Egoism? Why or why not?
3. Is the bank acting morally pursuant to Utilitarianism? Why or why not?
4. Is the bank acting morally pursuant to Kantian ethics? Why or why not?
5. What should a socially responsible bank be doing in China?
6. What should a leader who engages in sustainable leadership be doing regarding such recruitment practices in China?

## Bibliography

- Cavico, Frank J. and Mujtaba, Bahaudin G. (2011). *Baksheesh or Bribe: Cultural Conventions and Legal Pitfalls*. Davie, Florida: ILEAD Academy, LLC.
- Cavico, Frank J. and Mujtaba, Bahaudin G. (2013). *Business Ethics: The Moral Foundation for Effective Leadership, Management, and Entrepreneurship*. Boston, Massachusetts: Pearson Custom Publishing.
- Cavico, Frank J. and Mujtaba, Bahaudin G. (2014). *Legal Challenges for the Global Manager and Entrepreneur* (Second Edition). Dubuque, Iowa: Kendall-Hunt Publishing Company.
- Chow, Daniel (2012). The Interplay between China's Anti-Bribery Laws and the Foreign Corrupt Practices Act. *Ohio State Law Journal*, Vol. 73, pp. 1015-1037.
- Chow, Daniel, C.K. (May, 2014). Asia-Pacific Issue: Panel on China and the FCPA: Three Major Risks under the Foreign Corrupt Practices Act for U.S. Multinational Companies Doing Business in China. *Fordham International Law Journal*, Vol. 37, pp. 1183-1191.
- Curran, Enda and Eaglesham, Jean, "Regulators Step Up Probe Into Bank Hiring," *The Wall Street Journal*, May 8, 2014, pp. A1, A8.
- Glazer, Emily, Fitzpatrick, Dan, and Eaglesham, Jean, "J.P. Morgan Was Warned on Hiring," *The Wall Street Journal*, October 23, 2014, pp. C1, C2.
- Gorman, Thomas O. (May, 2014). Asia-Pacific Issue: Panel on China and the FCPA: Emerging Trends in FCPA Enforcement. *Fordham International Law Journal*, Vol. 37, pp.1193-1213.
- Holzer, Jessica and Johnson, Fawn, "Larger Bounties Spur Surge in Fraud Tips," *The Wall Street Journal*, September 7, 2010, p. C3.
- Jones, Ashby and Lublin, Joann S., "Critics Blow Whistle on Law," *The Wall Street Journal*, November 2, 2010, pp. B1, B11.
- Levin, Ned, Glazer, Emily, and Matthews, Christopher M., "Emails Track J.P. Morgan Hire in China," *The Wall Street Journal*, February 7, 2015, pp. A1, A8.
- Palazzolo, Joe, Matthews, Christopher M., and Ng, Serena, "Nepotism: When Is It a Crime"? *The Wall Street Journal*, August 20, 2013, pp. B1, B2.
- Protess, Ben and Silver-Greenberg, "On Defensive, JP Morgan Hired China's Elite," *The New York Times*, December 29, 2013. Retrieved January 10, 2015 from: http://dealbook.nytimes.com/2013/12/29/on-defensive-jpmorgan-hired-chinas-elite/.
- Runnels, Michael B. and Burton, Adam M. (October, 2012). The Foreign Corrupt Practices Act and New Governance: Incentivizing Ethical Foreign Direct Investment in China and Other Emerging Nations. *Cardozo Law Review*, Vol. 34, pp. 295-328.
- Silver-Greenberg, Protess, Ben, and Barboza, David, "Hiring in China by JP Morgan under scrutiny," *The Miami Herald*, August 18, 2013, p. 4A.

## 7.  Warnings on Pizza

*Bloomberg Businessweek* (2015) reported on a growing legal and ethical controversy regarding pizza and the national campaign against obesity, particularly childhood obesity. There is no doubt that people in the U.S. love to eat pizza as *Bloomberg Businessweek* (2015, p. 35) indicated that approximately 41 million Americans eat a slice of pizza every day. The U.S. government, specifically the Department of Agriculture, has also been encouraging Americans to eat more cheese pizza so as to increase their dairy consumption. As a result, *Bloomberg Businessweek* (2015) reported that in 2009 the Domino's pizza chain marketed an American Legends Pizza, which contains 40% more cheese. However, today, the pizza industry has now become a prime target in the U.S. fight against obesity.

Legally, the fight is occurring on two levels: common law civil actions for damages based on the tort of strict liability; and rulemaking by the federal U.S. Food and Drug Administration (FDA). Legal liability pursuant to strict liability can arise if there is no warning or an inadequate warning on a product, including a food product, which can cause harm, thereby rendering the product "defective" (Cavico and Mujtaba, 2014). Yet there is no legal duty to warn a consumer of risks that a reasonable and rational consumer should be aware of, for example, that a knife is sharp and can cut or that one can fall from a bicycle. So far, these common law legal actions have been unsuccessful.

There is, however, a great deal of legal activity on the federal regulatory level at the FDA as reported by *Bloomberg Businessweek* (2015). The FDA is an independent regulatory agency that has been empowered by Congress to make laws in the form of agency rules to regulate the food and drug industries to benefit the public interest. The FDA is in the process of finalizing rules requiring that pizza businesses post calorie information, like the burger chicken fast-food chains do. The response from the fast-food industry has been mixed. Some pizza chains and pizza businesses plan to fight the rules. Yet other fast-food businesses have taken the completely opposite approach and have joined the national battle against obesity by offering healthier options and informing the consumers accordingly. For example, *Bloomberg Businessweek* (2015) reported that McDonald's has taken soda out of its Happy Meals and also has added calorie counts to its menus. Moreover, Wendy's has taken soda off its children's menu. Furthermore, Olive Garden and Red Lobster have reduced the calorie count in children's meals and have made vegetables and milk side and drink options.

The pizza industry is taking a different approach and is fighting back. The industry's main lobbying and advocacy group is the American Pizza Community, which was formed in 2010 led by Domino's Pizza. The group represents the domestic pizza industry in the U.S., which is estimated to be valued at $37 billion. A principal goal of the lobbying group is to convince the agency as well as federal and state legislators that pizza is different from fast-food because it cannot be quickly made and thus pizza deserves special treatment (*Bloomberg Businessweek* (2015).

The FDA's proposed regulations, according to *Bloomberg Businessweek* (2015), would have required pizza businesses to post the calorie content by the whole pie as opposed to the slice, which proposal produced an immediate negative outcry from the pizza business. *Bloomberg Businessweek* (2015, p. 36) quoted the owner of a pizza business in suburban Chicago who expressed her concern that if a customer looked at the nutritional information on a large pizza box, menu, or display, and saw a 10,000 calorie figure, the customer might be reluctant to buy the pizza. Moreover, chain pizza companies contend that it would almost impossible to post accurate calorie counts due to the variety and range of toppings available, particularly in pizza businesses where most customers order for delivery. A compromise proposal offered would require the calorie content to be posted by slice only and to include only the standard toppings. Yet, the pizza industry says the compromise proposal would still be too great a burden on the smaller pizza businesses. If the FDA does adopt any rules, the pizza industry then says it will go to Congress to attempt to convince the legislators to overrule any agency rules perceived to be too burdensome. *Bloomberg Businessweek* (2015) reported that over the last two federal election cycles the pizza industry has contributed approximately $1.3 million to Republicans, whereas Democrats received only about $157,000. Yet another legal issue will be if the proposed rules apply to frozen pizza, which industry also has been battling the FDA over proposed rules. At issue is whether pizza should be considered as vegetable, especially for school lunch programs, due to the tomato paste, as well as how much sodium and whole grain can be used in pizza dough. *Bloomberg Businessweek* (2015, p. 36) quoted the head of another lobbying group, the National Frozen Pizza Institution, who warned against regulating the pizza industry, declaring that pizza is the "greatest food in America" and "part of America, and it has been for a long time."

### *Bibliography*:
- Cavico, Frank J. and Mujtaba, Bahaudin, G. (2014). *Legal Challenges for the Global Manager and Entrepreneur* (Second Edition). Dubuque, Iowa: Kendall-Hunt Publishing Company.
- Lobbying, "Making Washington Fall in Love with Pizza Again," *Bloomberg Businessweek*, March 16-27, 2015, pp. 35-36.

### *Questions for Discussion:*
1. Is a pizza legally "defective" under strict liability law because it does not contain a warning as to the calorie content of the pie or slice? Why or why not, and if so what should the warning say and should it apply to the whole pie or slice? And if there is liability, how does one go about proving that the lack of the warning caused the harm, that is, the consumer's obesity?
2. What should the FDA's final rules be? Why? Should pizza be classified as a vegetable for school lunch purposes? Why or why not?

3.  From the vantage point of Ethical Egoism, how should an egoistic and self-interested pizza industry deal with the FDA's proposed rulemaking? Should the industry fight or compromise, and if the latter, how?
4.  Is the sale of pizza without the calorie information moral pursuant to the ethical theories of Utilitarianism and Kantian ethics? Why or why not?
5.  What should a socially responsible pizza industry be doing for the communities where it does business, for the consumer, and for society as a whole?
6.  How should a leader who engages in sustainable leadership respond to this pizza warning controversy?

## 8. Chinese "Birth Tourism"

In 2015, federal government agents in Los Angeles and several other Southern California cities conducted an investigation, including executing search warrants, in an attempt to crackdown on maternity tourism, also called "birth tourism," principally perpetrated by Chinese nationals. The focus of the investigation was on maternity tour operators who arrange for pregnant Chinese women to come to the U.S. to give birth to their children, who then automatically become U.S. citizens by being born here. People from many different countries, particularly China, but also South Korea and people from the Middle East and Africa, as well as people from Mexico, have engaged in "birth tourism," but recently there has been a great deal of tourist activity – legitimate and otherwise - from mainland China by wealthy Chinese. Yet many wealthy foreigners – again from China and elsewhere, are allowed to come to the U.S. on non-immigrant visitor visas for tourism and business purposes as well as medical care.

There is no prohibition on pregnant women travelling to the U.S on tourist visas or otherwise, but it is illegal to misrepresent the purpose of one's trip to immigration authorities when applying for a visa and entering the country. Nevertheless, in two years, more than 400 American babies of Chinese national origin were born in Orange County, California, hospitals, resulting in hundreds of thousands of dollars for just one "birth tourism" business. The residences were the Chinese live until they go to the hospital are called "Chinese birthing houses" or "maternity hotels."

The motive for the Chinese national is apparent; their children will be U.S. citizens, who can petition eventually for their parents to become permanent residents and then ultimately citizens too. Their children will be automatically eligible for top-notch U.S. universities in California and throughout the U.S., including paying in-state tuition in California. Furthermore, if conditions deteriorate in China, having children as U.S. citizens will provide an alternative life for the whole family. But lying to immigration to obtain a visa under false pretenses is illegal. In one instance reported in the news, federal agents raided an apartment complex in Irvine, California, located in Orange County. Federal agents stated that the apartment complex housed a "birth tourism" business that charged pregnant women $50,000 for lodging, food, and transportation. Lodging typically lasts three months before and three months after the birth of the child. Wealthy Chinese have paid up to $80,000 to have their children born here. The government agents asserted that the Chinese women were instructed to lie about their travel plans when they applied for tourist visas. Moreover, government agents said that the women were promised Social Security numbers and passports for their babies before they returned to China. Also, it was asserted that the "birth tourism" operators told the women to fly to California via Hawaii, where the customs and immigration officers were supposedly more lenient to immigrants than in California.

Chinese "birth tourism" businesses advertise openly on the Internet and in Chinese publications. The businesses promise to obtain a birth certificate, passport, and social security number for the new-born Chinese. A "full package" also includes transportation to and from the airport, visits to grocery stores and restaurants, including upscale ones, entertainment, including going to Disney, and, most importantly, pre-natal visits to doctors. The Chinese, moreover, are coached what to say and how to act and how to keep a low profile. When in the hospital, the women are told to tell the hospital personnel that they are indigent, thereby meaning that the cost of the birth of their babies, up to $25,000, will be borne by the U.S. government (that is, the taxpayers). The women then return to China with their U.S. born and citizen babies, often called "anchor babies." However, the businesses advise women not to apply for a visa if they are too visibly pregnant. One business was reportedly able to earn hundreds of thousands of dollars in income for this type of visa fraud. And one company promises to refund any money paid if the women are denied a visa.

As of the writing of this case study, no arrests have been made and no charges have been filed, and the government is still investigating. However, U.S. Customs and Immigration are now looking closely at Chinese "tourists" at the consulates overseas and at the border. Specifically, U.S. officials are asking certain key questions, to wit: Is a woman pregnant? When is her due date? What are her travel plans? And what medical insurance does she have? The objective is to determine whether the women are committing visa fraud and thus whether they can legally enter the country. One immigration activist condemned Chinese "birth tourism" as "citizenship for sale." In order to prevent "birth tourism" and "anchor babies," U.S. Senator David Vitter (R.-La.) introduced a bill in the Senate that would not allow a child born to a foreigner in the U.S. to become a U.S. citizen automatically unless one parent is a U.S. citizen, a lawful permanent resident, or is in the military.

***Bibliography:***
- Jordan, Miriam, "Birth-Tourism Spots Raided," *The Wall Street Journal*, March 4, 1015, p. A3.
- La Juenesse, William and Prabucki, Laura, "Feds crack down on Chinese 'birth tourism.'" *FOX News*, March 3, 2015. Retrieved March 3, 2015 from: http://www.foxnews.com/us/2015/03/03/feds-crack-down-on-chinese-birth-tourism-scam.

- Taxin, Amy, "Agents crack down on maternity tourism ring," *Sun-Sentinel*, March 4, 2015, p. 3D.

### *Questions for Discussion:*
1. Discuss the legal implications of Chinese "birth tourism." What factors would indicate visa fraud?
2. Is Chinese "birth tourism" moral pursuant to Ethical Egoism, Ethical Relativism, Utilitarianism, and Kantian ethics? Why or why not?
3. Is Senator Vitter's bill a moral one pursuant to Ethical Egoism, Ethical Relativism, Utilitarianism, and Kantian ethics? Why or why not?
4. What should a socially responsible Chinese "birth tourism" business be doing for the local community?

## 9. Kraft - Heinz Food Merger

In 2015, Kraft Foods Group announced it would merge with H.J. Heinz Company in a $49 billion deal. The merger will create the third-largest food/beverage company in North America and the fifth largest worldwide; Kraft on its own is the fourth largest food-maker in North America (Wohl, 2015). The new company will be called the Kraft Heinz Company; it will be publicly traded; and it will have a market value of more than $80 billion (Gelles, 2015).

The merged company will now have a wide variety of very well-known products, ranging from Heinz Ketchup, Jell-O, Kraft Macaroni and Cheese, Cool-Whip dessert topping, Maxwell House coffee, Velvetta cheese, to Philadelphia Cream Cheese. Kraft's products could benefit from the merger since Heinz has a very large presence outside the United States, whereas Kraft is heavily focused on the U.S. food market. The *New York Times* (Gelles, 2015, p. B3) pointed out that "Kraft ...sells almost all of its products in the United States." About 61% of Heinz's sales are already outside of North America, including 25% of sales to emerging markets, the *Miami Herald* (Wohl, 2015) reported. The merger is thus viewed as an opportunity for Kraft to grow internationally.

Kraft's business has been slow to grow, perhaps because many younger consumers are demonstrating a preference for natural and organic ingredients, as well as fresher and healthier products, which latest trend Kraft is attempting to adjust to (Cimiluca, Mattoli, and Gasparro, 2015). The *Wall Street Journal* (Cimiluca, Mattoli, and Gasparro. 2015, p. A1) pointed out that "Kraft and many other U.S. packaged-food giants have struggled with rapid changes in consumer tastes that have curbed sales and exposed overcapacity." The *New York Times* (Gelles, 2015, p. B1) pointed out that "millennials and affluent consumers are seeking more organic, fresh, and local products. Lower income consumers are spending less on name brands." However, "Kraft has attempted to adapt its products to shifting tastes, such as by taking artificial coloring out of its macaroni and cheese" (Cimiluca, Mattoli, and Gasparro, 2015 p. A6). The *New York Times*

(Gelles, 2015) predicted that the merger will allow the companies to introduce more healthy versions of some of their strong brands.

The *Wall Street Journal* (Cimiluca, Mattoli, and Gasparro, 2015, p. A6) noted that in 2014 Kraft's revenue was "effectively flat" at $18 billion, while net profits fell 62% to $1 billion. Combined, the revenue for the merged companies would be about $28 billion (Kesmodel and Gasparro, 2015). The company will have dual headquarters in Chicago and Pittsburg. The current chairman of Heinz, Alex Behring, who is also a managing partner of 3G Capital, which helped to orchestrate the merger, will become chairman of the board of the new company. And John Cahill, the Kraft chairman will become vice-chairman. The current Heinz chief executive officer, Bernardo Hees, will also remain as CEO of the merged company. The combined company will have 46,000 employees.

The merger was accomplished by 3G Capital and Warren Buffet's Berkshire Hathaway, which will invest $10 billion in the new business. 3G Capital is a private equity firm founded by Brazilian billionaire, Jorge Paulo Lemann. Buffet and Lemann had previously joined together to purchase Heinz in 2013 for $23 billion (Cimiluca, Mattoli, and Gasparro, 2015), where they cut costs, which is a strategy they are expected to implement again with the merger (Giammona and Boyle, 2015). The *Wall Street Journal* (Cimiluca, Mattoli, and Gasparro, 2015, p. A6) indicated that "3G uses a process called 'zero-coast budgeting,' in which each division of a company must justify its costs from scratch each year. Shortly after acquiring Heinz, for instance, 3G moved to close plants across the country and eliminated more than 1000 jobs." The *Wall Street Journal* (Kesmodel and Gasparro, 2015, p. A6) further explained that "zero-based budgeting requires managers to plan each year's budget as if no money existed the previous year, rather than using the typical method of adjusting prior year spending. That forces them to justify the costs and benefits of each dollar every 12 months. So, for example, once-successful divisions that have fizzled can't keep spending like they did in their hey-day." At Heinz, management positions were particularly hard hit; corporate jets were eliminated; and employees had to get permission to make photo copies (Kesmodel and Gasparro, 2015). Commentators (Giammona and Boyle, 2015; Wohl, 2015) reported that the companies are expected to reduce annual costs by$1.5 billion to $2 billion by the end of 2017. Regarding the cost reductions and efficiencies of scale expected to result from the merger, according to the *New York Times* (Gelles, 2015, B3), "much of that could come from cutting jobs, something 3G is known to do after acquiring companies." Berkshire Hathaway and 3G Capital also teamed up in 2014 when 3G, which owns Burger King, acquired the Canadian coffee-and-donut chain, Tim Hortons, Inc. The *Wall Street Journal* ((Cimiluca, Mattoli, and Gasparro, 2015) noted that the Campbell Soup company is supposed to be another 3G acquisition target.

Heinz shareholders, including Warren Buffet's Berkshire Hathaway, in addition to 3G Capital, will hold a 51% share of the new merged company. Kraft shareholders will receive 49% of the stock in the combined company, as well as a special cash dividend of $6.50 a share. The *Wall Street Journal* reported that Kraft's stock prices "soared" 36% on the merger news (Kesmodel and Gasparro, 2015, p. A1). The merger could produce more consolidation in the food industry in the United States, which is struggling to regain growth (Giammona and Boyle, 2015). The *Wall Street Journal* (Kesmodel and Gasparro, 2015, p. A6) explained that "big packaged-food companies have been particularly appealing targets for zero-based budgeting. Many of them are fighting rapid shifts in consumer tastes away from processed foods such as Cheez Whiz and Ore-Ida Bagel Bites towards items deemed fresher or healthier. That's sapped growth and made the companies ripe for cost cuts."

The U.S. Federal Trade Commission (FTC) must approve the merger. The key law is the merger test in the 1914 Clayton Anti-trust Act. Pursuant to that statute, a merger will not be approved by the government if there is a reasonable probability of a substantial lessening of competition or the tendency to create a monopoly (defined as a company having a 70% or more market share) in a relevant market (Cavico and Mujtaba, 2014). Defining the pertinent "market" is a critical feature in U.S. anti-trust law, particularly under merger law. Most interestingly, the *Miami Herald* (Wohl, 2015, p. 3C) quoted an anti-trust expert who said that in the past the Federal Trade Commission has taken a "narrow" approach in evaluating food product mergers. That is, food product mergers would be evaluated in "narrow categories", meaning that there might be an overlap of some products by the merged companies and few other competitors, thereby perhaps causing a lessening of competition in a narrowly defined market (Wohl, 2015). To illustrate, in the past the Federal Trade Commission has defined markets very narrowly, for example, as "premium ice cream" and "super intense mints" (Wohl, 2015).

### *Bibliography:*

- Cavico, Frank J. and Mujtaba, Bahaudin G. (2014). *Legal Challenges for the Global Manager and Entrepreneur* (Second Edition). Dubuque, Iowa: Kendall Hunt Publishing Company.
- Cimilluca, Dana, Mattoli, Dana, and Gasparro, Annie, "Brazil's 3G in Serious Talks with Kraft," *The Wall Street Journal*, March 25, 2015, pp. A1, A6.
- Gelles, David, "A Mega-Bet on Processed Food," *The New York Times*, March 26, 2015, pp. B1, B3.
- Giammona, Craig and Boyle, Matthew, "Kraft to merge with Heinz in huge deal," *Sun-Sentinel*, March 26, 2015, pp. 1D, 4D.
- Kesmodel, David and Gasparro, Annie, "Lean Recipe Fuels Food Deals," *The Wall Street Journal*, March 26, 2015, pp. A1, A6.
- Wohl, Jessica, "Heinz buying Kraft to build $28 B food giant," *Miami Herald*, March 26, 2015, pp. 1C, 3C.

### *Questions for Discussion:*

1. Is the Kraft - Heinz food merger a legal one pursuant to the merger test in the Clayton Anti-trust Act? Why or why not? How would you define the pertinent

"market"? Why? Should the market be defined as narrowly as the Federal Trade Commission has done in the past? Why or why not?

2. Is the merger a moral one pursuant to the doctrine of Ethical Egoism? Why or why not?
3. Is the merger a moral one pursuant to Utilitarian ethics? Why or why not?
4. Is the merger a moral one pursuant to Kantian ethics? Why or why not?
5. What should a socially responsible giant food company be doing for the communities where it does business and for society as a whole?
6. How should a leader who engages in sustainable leadership respond to any government challenge of the merger?

## 10. Verizon – AOL Merger

In 2015, Verizon Communications, Inc., the largest wireless provider in the United States, announced its intent to purchase AOL, Inc. in a merger valued at $4.4 billion. The objective of the merger is for Verizon to integrate its wireless network with advertising and content programming. Verizon currently has more than 100 million monthly wireless subscribers. However, the company and also other phone companies are under a great deal of pressure as growth in their core wireless businesses has slowed. But Verizon also has a growing cable television business. The merger means that Verizon will be attempting to obtain new revenue sources beyond the call and data services it now sells to its wireless subscribers. Verizon clearly wants to expand into digital and video platforms. AOL.com is the 41st most visited website in the United States. AOL owns such websites as the Huffington Post (which is the 30th most visited website in the U.S.) and TechCrunch, which appeal to younger people; and Verizon has expanded its mobile content over the years. About 2.1 million people still use AOL's dial-up service. AOL has a great deal of video content. Purchasing AOL will place Verizon in the business of selling more video but also embedding ads in videos that appear on the Web. Moreover, AOL has advanced technology for selling ads by means of its ad tech program and delivering high-quality Web video. A part of AOL that Verizon found very appealing is called AOL's "programmatic advertising business," which is a system that matches online advertisers with consumers across different platforms, and which collects valuable data throughout the process. Verizon thus believes that video will be a primary driver of demand for its wireless business. The company currently has an arrangement with the NFL that allows Verizon to stream some games over the phone for free. A major objective of the merger, therefore, is to make Verizon's own phone and Internet offerings more appealing to consumers.

Verizon will pay $50 a share, which was a 17% premium over AOL's stock price shortly before the merger announcement. AOL's shares jumped to $50.52; but Verizon's shares went down 0.4% to $49.62. The deal is funded by all cash and commercial paper. In 2014, AOL generated revenue of approximately $2.5 billion, which was about 9% higher than the previous year, and a profit of $126 million. The CEO of the merged company will be Verizon's CEO, Lowell

McAdam. Under his leadership the company has made substantial investments in video. AOL will become a division of Verizon. AOL's CEO Tim Armstrong, who was a former Google executive, will continue to head AOL's operations after the merger is completed. Under his leadership, AOL has invested heavily in ad technology. In 2013, AOL purchased Adapt.tv, which is an exchange that connects buyers and sellers of online video advertising. Now that purchase is considered to be a very shrewd move by Armstrong. Tim Armstrong stands to gain almost $180 million from the merger since he owns 6.7% of AOL. He also has stock options with AOL that Verizon will honor as part of the merger but he will have to wait a year after the merger closes to exercise those options. In 2014, his total compensation was $6.9 million, including a base salary of $1 million. Tim Armstrong has stated that the future of nearly all media, and thus the future of nearly all advertising, is "about our phones." He explained that more people now use their phones to connect to the Internet as opposed to their computers. More consumers are now watching videos – from YouTube to HBO – on their mobile phones. Regarding the employees, no major layoffs are expected; and AOL CEO Tim Armstrong said specifically that not only would AOL employees would be kept on, but that they would be kept on at their current salaries. All AOL media businesses would continue to operate, Armstrong said.

Verizon presently confronts increasing competition for its main wireless business, especially from T-Mobile US, Inc. AT&T, another big rival, is acquiring Direc-TV's satellite business. Comcast has agreed to buy NBCUniversal. One effect of the merger will be to increase the competition for advertising on mobile devices. By means of the deal, Verizon will get two key AOL technologies: its exclusive video content and its ability to automatically send targeted ads to mobile devices. Verizon, in the latter part of 2015, plans to introduce its mobile streaming service that features live television, original shows, and pay-per-view shows. The merger will also see Verizon emerging as a competitor against the two leading Web ad companies – Google, Inc. and Facebook, Inc. Currently, Google dominates the mobile advertising market. Together, Google and Facebook control more than 55% of the $42.6 billion worldwide mobile ad market. Verizon thus should emerge as a competitor in the rapidly emerging connected TV, mobile media, and advertising sectors. The company's goal is to sell more content, especially bundles of content, and to sell more ads through its wireless phone network.

The *Wall Street Journal* (Gryta and Marshall, 2015, pp. A1, A10) said that Verizon is "betting that Americans want to use their phones and Internet to watch more videos." Similarly, one business professor, who was quoted in the *New York Times* (Manjoo, 2015, p. B6), succinctly explained the rationale for the merger: "They know that mobile is where it's at if you want to get millennials." However, the professor also said that Verizon and AOL still "need to figure out this market" (Manjoo, 2015, p. B6).The merger must obtain government regulatory approval in the United States. The two agencies involved will be the Federal Trade Commission (FTC) and the Federal Communications Commission (FCC). The FTC will apply the merger standard in the Clayton Anti-trust Act. That statute states that a merger will not be approved if it there is a reasonable probability of a substantial lessening of competition or the tendency to create a monopoly in a relevant market. The definition of the pertinent "market" is critical under the Clayton Act. The legal standard that the FCC uses is a very general one, to wit: whether the communications merger is in the "public interest, convenience, or necessity."

*Bibliography:*
- Fox Business, *Dow Jones Newswires,* "Verizon to Acquire AOL in $4.4 Billion Deal," May 12, 2015, Retrieved May 12, 2015 from: http://www.foxbusiness.com/industries/2015/05/12/verizon-to-acquire-aol-in440billion-deal.
- Gelles, David, "Verizon Bets on Video Ads In $4 Billion Deal for AOL," *New York Times,* May 13, 2015, pp. B1, B6.
- Gryta, Thomas and Marshall, Jack, "Betting on the Future, Verizon Dials Up AOL," *Wall Street Journal,* May 13, 2015, pp. A1, A10.
- Manjo, Farhad, "Mobile Is Now a Magic Word," *New York Times,* May 13, 2015, pp. B1, B6.
- Moritz, Scott, "Verizon buys AOL in $4.4B mobile video push," *Miami Herald,* May 13, 2015, pp. 1C, 3C.
- Muskus, Jeff (Editor), "Verizon's AOL Deal Isn't About the News," Deals, *Bloomberg Businessweek,* May 18-24, 2015, pp. 35-36.
- Rooney, Ben, "Verizon buys AOL for $4.4 billion," *CNN Money,* May 12, 2015. Retrieved May 12, 2015 from: http://money.cnn.com/2015/05/12/investing/verion-buys-aol/index.html.
- Sharma, Amol, "$180 Million for AOL Boss," *Wall Street Journal,* May 14, 2015, p. B1.

*Questions for Discussion:*
1. Is the merger a legal one pursuant to the Clayton Act? Why or why not?
2. Is the merger a legal one pursuant to the FCC standard? Why or why not?
3. Is the merger a moral one pursuant to Ethical Egoism? Why or why not?
4. Is the merger a moral one pursuant to Utilitarianism? Why or why not?
5. Is the merger a moral one pursuant to Kantian ethics?
6. What should a socially and environmentally responsible merged company be doing for the communities where it does business and for society as a whole?
7. Do you agree with Tim Armstrong that the future of nearly all media and consequently nearly all advertising is "about our phones"? Why or why not?

# 11. Staples – Office Depot Merger

In 2015, Staples, Inc., the number one office supply retailer in the U.S., announced that it planned to buy its rival and number two office supply retailer, Office Depot, for $6.3 billion. The reason for the merger was that the union of the two former rivals would allow the merged company to compete better against giant retailers who sell office supplies, like Wal-Mart, as well as online sellers, such as Amazon. A combined distribution and sales network will help the merged company compete better against Wal-Mart and Amazon, which is the number one online seller.

Office Depot is based in Boca Raton, Florida; and Staples is based in Framingham, Massachusetts. If the merger is approved, Staples' current home is very likely expected to be the headquarters of the merged company. Ron Sargent is the CEO of Staples; and Roland Smith is the CEO of Office Depot. The combined company will have 4000 stores. The companies had already announced before the merger that they would close about 350 stores. Staples will increase the size of its board of directors from 11 to 13 by adding two of Office Depot's directors. Ron Sargent is expected to be the CEO of the merged company.

The two companies presently control more than 70% of the $197 billion office-supply market. Annual sales of the combined company are expected to be about $39 billion. The combined company is also expected to achieve $1 billion in cost savings from the merger. Office Depot's sales have been going down since 2007; and Staple's sales have been going down since 2011. Currently, 45% of the office-supply business revenue comes from office supplies and equipment, but Staples and Office Depot also sell computers, printers, and other electronics, as well as furniture, and thus they also compete with Best Buy and Costco. Moreover, the *Sun-Sentinel* reports that recently Staples has been moving toward selling a larger variety of supplies, for example, restaurant, medical office, and party supplies, and even school uniforms (Pounds, 2015). Staples is the number 3 online seller, behind Amazon and Apple, and Office Depot is number nine. Combined, Staples and Office Depot generated about $14.5 billion in online sales in 2013.

As to layoffs, they are expected, said the *New York Times* (Merced and Gelles, 2015), but there is no word yet on exact numbers. However, the *Sun-Sentinel* (Pounds, March 25, 2015) reported that if the merger is approved by the government, Office Depot's five top executives would receive payouts totaling $85 million, including a $46.78 million "golden parachute" for Chairman and Chief Executive, Roland Smith, who was named to the top position in November of 2013. The amount to Smith includes $39.29 million in stock and $7.47 million as a lump-sum cash severance. Staples will pay $7.25 per share in cash and 0.2188 of its shares for each Office Depot share, which price was a premium of 44% to Office Depot's close before the announcement was made. Initially, the price of Staples stock fell about 10%, due in large part to anti-trust concerns, but the price of Office Depot stock increased about 1.5%. One analyst quoted in *Reuters News* said that Staples is paying "more than a fair price" for Office Depot; and the analyst also said that Staples was taking on a large debt to buy a rival in a weak market (Reuters, 2015). Hedge fund Starboard Value owns 5% of Staples and 10% of Office Depot. The *Sun-Sentinel* (Pounds, 2015) indicated that the hedge fund was actively advocating the merger, expecting that it would benefit investors in the long-term.

The U.S. Federal Trade Commission (FTC) must approve the merger. The key law is the merger test in the 1914 Clayton Act. Pursuant to that statute, a merger will not be approved by the government if there is a reasonable probability of a substantial lessening of competition or the tendency to create a monopoly (defined as a company having a 70% or more market share) in a relevant market (Cavico and Mujtaba, 2014). Defining the pertinent "market" is a critical feature in U.S. anti-trust law, particularly under merger law. Recall that in 1997 the Federal Trade Commission ruled against the then proposed merger of Office Depot and Staples; and a federal court judge agreed with the FTC, thereby ending the merger at that time. Then, the FTC decided that the pertinent "market" for anti-trust purposes pursuant to the Clayton Act was small, encompassing only office supply super-stores, of which there were three. And thus when number one at the time, Office Depot, planned to merge with number two, Staples, the federal judge said that the result would be anti-competitive leaving only a "dwarfish," the judge said, Office Max. Yet in 2013, the FTC approved the merger of Office Depot and Office Max. What had changed? According the FTC, the pertinent "market" had changed. The market was more broadly construed as any store selling office supplies, including such giants as Costco, Wal-Mart, Target, as well as online retailers, such as Amazon, and not just office supply super-stores. The *Wall Street Journal* (Kendall, 2015) pointed out that in 2013 the FTC's rationale for approving the merger was, according to agency studies, that fewer consumers went to office supply superstores to shop for office supplies; rather, more consumers were going to other large retail stores to buy their office supplies as well as many other kinds of products. Moreover, the *Wall Street Journal* found that office supply super stores were losing substantial in-store sales to online competitors. The *Miami Herald* also emphasized that many consumers now are much more comfortable shopping online, including for office supplies (Chapman and D'Innocenzio, 2015). The FTC also found that in the Office Depot- Office Max merger that each company had little impact on the other's in-store pricing since there were many other competitors in the market that competed effectively to serve medium- and small-sized businesses (Fitzgerald and Hoffman, 2015). The *Miami Herald* also pointed out that consumers are now buying smaller technical devices, such as Smartphones, as opposed to personal computers, which along with ink and cartridges have been "bread-and-butter" items for the office supply superstores (Chapman and D'Innocenzio, 2015). To illustrate, the *Miami Herald* related that in 2014 $9.2 billion was spent buying office products online, which was 24% of the office supply market; and those figures rose from 2004 where $2.6 billion was spent, accounting for 7% of the market (Chapman and D'Innocenzio, 2015).

Accordingly, the *Wall Street Journal* quoted an anti-trust lawyer who said that the FTC's 2013 rationales would carry over to the present merger (Kendall, 2015, p. B3). Similarly, *Reuters News* quoted a former attorney in the anti-trust division of the Justice Department who said that the same factors the FTC stated and relied on in the Office Depot – Office Max merger are also present for the Staples – Office Depot merger (Reuters, 2015). It is also important to point out that in the Office Depot – Office Max merger the FTC did not require the merged company to divest any stores, which may not be the case with the current merger.

However, the *Wall Street Journal* also noted that for the present merger the FTC wants to investigate how the merger would affect large business customers, as well as medium-sized ones, who buy office supplies from the two companies on a regular contract basis (Kendall, 2015). The distinction between the retail market and the big business and government market will be a factor that will "loom large" in the FTC's deliberations, said the *Wall Street Journal* (Fitzgerald and Hoffman, 2015, p. B1). Another potential factor affecting the Staples – Office Depot merger, which the FTC also will investigate, would be whether prices for office supplies have risen since the Office Depot – Office Max merger. And another factor will be whether customers, especially large ones, can buy supplies directly from the manufacturers. It is also pertinent to point out that Radio Shack declared for bankruptcy right after the merger announcement, as apparently that company could not compete against bigger and more low-cost competitors, including online ones. The merger will also be reviewed by the anti-trust division of the European Commission, which has been known to take a strict construction of anti-trust laws (Pounds, 2015). The merger clearly will be closely evaluated by the FTC and the European Commission due to the basic fact that the number of office supply super-stores will have been reduced to a single one. The *New York Times* (Merced and Gelles, 2015, p. B3) quoted a co-founder of Staples who said to expect a "long and nasty legal skirmish."

*Bibliography:*

- Cavico, Frank J. and Mujtaba, Bahaudin G. (2014). *Legal Challenges for the Global Manager and Entrepreneur* (Second Edition). Dubuque, Iowa: Kendall Hunt Publishing Company.
- Chapman, Michelle and D'Innocenzio, Anne, "Staples to buy Office Depot for $6B," *Miami Herald*, February 5, 2015, p. C1.
- Fitzgerald, Drew and Hoffman, Liz, "Staples Inks Merger, FTC Calculates Fallout," *Wall Street Journal*. February 5, 2015, pp. B1, B2.
- Kendall, Brent, "Staples – Office Depot Deal Would Test U.S. Regulators, *Wall Street Journal*, February 4, 2015, p. B3.
- Merced, Michael J. de la, and Gelles, David, "Office Retailers Say a Merger Will Keep Them Competitive." *New York Times*, February 5, 2015, p. B3.
- Pounds, Marcia Heroux, "Antitrust questions in merger," *Sun-Sentinel*, February 7, 2015, pp. 1D, 4D.
- Pounds, Marcia Heroux, "Top execs to earn $85M from merger," *Sun-Sentinel*, March 25, 2015, pp. 1D, 4D.
- Reuters, "Staples Snags Rival Office Depot for $6.3 Billion," *Fox Business*, February 4, 2015. Retrieved February 4, 2015 from: http://www.foxbusiness.com/inudstries/2015.02/04/staples-snags-rival-office-depot-for-63-billion

*Questions:*
1. Is the Staples – Office Depot merger legal pursuant to the anti-trust merger test in the Clayton Act? What is the relevant market? Has the market changed from the previous attempt at a merger? Has the FTC, in essence, "boxed" itself in by its prior approval of the Office Depot – Office Max merger? How and why is the determination of the market critical in this case?
2. Is the Staples - Office Depot merger a moral one pursuant to Ethical Egoism from the vantage point of the two companies? Why or why not?
3. Is the merger a moral one pursuant to Utilitarian ethics? Why or why not?
4. Is the merger a moral one pursuant to Kantian ethics? Why or why not?
5. What should a socially and environmentally responsible merged company be doing for the local community where it does business and for society as a whole?
6. How should a leader who engages in sustainable leadership respond to any government opposition to the merger?

## 12. Disney and the H-1B Visa Program

The *Miami Herald* (Preston, 2015) presented a picture of a very controversial practice at Walt Disney World – the layoffs of employees who were replaced by immigrants on temporary visas used for highly skilled technical workers. In 2014, 250 Disney employees, who apparently were performing very well at their jobs monitoring computers for reservations, ticket sales, and store purchases, were laid off. Moreover, many of their jobs were transferred to immigrants on temporary visas for highly skilled technical workers, who were brought in by an outsourcing firm based in India. Furthermore, over the next three months some Disney employees were required to train their replacements to do the jobs that they had lost. The *Miami Herald* quoted one laid-off employee, an American male in his 40s, who still remains unemployed, who said it was "humiliating" to train someone else to take over one's job (Preston, 2015, p. 1L). Disney responded by saying that the lay-offs were part of a "reorganization" designed to foster "innovation" and that the company created more jobs than it eliminated, specifically achieving a net gain of 70 tech jobs. The *Miami Herald* reported that Disney told the laid-off workers that certain positions were eliminated as a result of work being transitioned to a "managed service provider" (Preston, 2015, p. 4L). Severance packages were offered as well as a "stay bonus," representing 10% of severance, if the laid-off employees remained for 90 days and performed satisfactorily, which, according to the *Miami Herald* (Preston, 2015), meant training their young Indian immigrant replacements.

Currently, there is a debate in the U.S. Congress about whether the H-1B visa program, which are temporary visas, but can be renewed, and which are used to place immigrants in high-tech jobs in the U.S., should be curtailed, eliminated, or, as the tech companies contend, expanded due to the shortage of workers in high-tech fields. Presently, there are 85,000 visas allotted each year; and they are in high demand. Tech giants like Microsoft, Google, and Facebook have been lobbying Congress to increase the number of H-1B visas, saying that there are not enough U.S. workers with the specialized skills they need. Many U.S. companies use the visa program, but, according to the *Miami Herald* (Preston, 2015) the largest recipients of the visas are outsourcing or consulting firms based in India, or their U.S. subsidiaries, which bring workers to the U.S. on large contracts to, in essence, take over entire in-house technology units, primarily to reduce costs. The immigrants are technically the employees of the outsourcing or consulting companies. In 2013, reported the *Miami Herald* (Preston, 2015), the top firms were Tata Consultancy Services, Infosys, and HCL American, which was the company hired by Disney. Each one of the aforementioned companies received more than 1000 visas each. One critic of the visa program, related the *Miami Herald*, told members of Congress at a hearing that the immigrants work for less than U.S. workers, and in some cases companies have saved 25 to 49 percent of wage costs (Preston, 2015, p. 1L). Accordingly, Congress continues to investigate lay-offs purportedly driven by the visa program.

Officially, as per federal guidelines, the visas are intended to be granted to foreigners with advanced scientific and computer skills in order to fill positions when U.S. workers cannot be found. Their use, moreover, according to the federal guidelines, should not adversely affect the wages and working conditions of U.S. workers. However, the *Miami Herald* (Preston, 2015, p. 1L) said there are "loopholes" in the law, and consequently as a practical matter companies do not have to recruit U.S. workers first or even guarantee that a U.S worker will not be displaced. Critics of the visa program also contend that the visas are being used to bring in foreign workers who will do the same work as U.S. workers but for less money, and with the laid-off U.S workers doing the training of their replacements. One laid-off Disney worker, age 57, was quoted in the *Miami Herald* (Preston, 2015, p. 4L), saying that he was forced into early retirement and that the whole situation was "horrible." He is still looking for another job.

### *Bibliography:*
- Preston, Julia, "H-1B visas in spotlight amid layoffs at Disney," *Miami Herald*, July 7, 2015, pp. 1L, 4L.

### *Questions for Discussion:*
1. Discuss the legal issues that could arise in a company's use of the H-1B visa program? How should these issues be resolved?
2. Even if legal, is the H-1B visa program moral pursuant to Ethical Egoism, Utilitarianism, and Kantian ethics? Why or why not?
3. What should a socially responsible company be doing to rectify the apparent shortage of highly skilled U.S. workers?
4. How should a leader who engages in sustainable leadership respond to the apparent shortage of highly skilled U.S. workers?

## 13. Advertising "Imported" Beer Made in America

The *Wall Street Journal* (Gershman and Mickle, 2015) on a controversy regarding allegedly deceptive advertising by beer manufacturers who are accused of misleading consumers to thinking that their beer is imported, but in reality it is made in the U.S.A The leading case, which was based on state law, and which resulted in a settlement, involved Beck's beer, which is owned by the giant liquor manufacturer, InBev. A class-action lawsuit accused Beck of deceiving U.S. consumers into believing that the beer was authentic German beer imported from Germany, although the beer was really brewed in St. Louis. As a result of the settlement of the lawsuit, consumers of Beck's beer who purchased the beer after 2011, and who can produce valid receipts can get a refund of up to $50. Specifically, Beck's drinkers can get 10 cents back for every individual bottle purchased, 50 cents for a six-pack, or $1.25 for a 20-package. There is an online form to claim a refund. Four law firms involved in the lawsuit will get $3.5 million in legal fees and costs. Also, as part of the settlement, Beck's agreed to make adjustments to its advertising, labelling, and packaging. Specifically, a statement on the bottle saying that the beer is made in the U.S.A. will become more visible. Moreover, the green boxes win which the bottles are packaged also will specify that the beer in made in the U.S.A.

The production of Beck's beer moved from Germany to St. Louis in 2012. However, the advertising, including on the packaging, continued to say that the beer was "German Quality Beer" and "Originated in Bremen, Germany." The lawsuit, which was based on state consumer protection law, stated that the company misled consumers by giving them a false impression as to where the beer was made. Beck's, however, is not the only beer manufacturer to be involved in an advertising controversy, the *Wall Street Journal* reported. For example, Red Stripe beer, which is owned by Diageo PLC, advertises itself as a "Jamaican-style Lager"; Foster's, made by Miller-Coors, uses a kangaroo in its advertising and packaging to emphasize its Australian heritage; and Killian's Irish Red refers to its Irish roots in its name; yet all these beers are brewed in the U.S.A. However, significantly, all also say on their packaging that the beers are brewed in the U.S.A. In the case of Foster's beer, a company spokesperson, reported the *Wall Street Journal*, stated that the decision to brew the beer in the U.S.A. was driven by costs, especially since that brand comes in 25 ounce cans which are heavy and expensive to ship; thus, the beer is made at the Miller-Coors brewery in Ft. Worth, Texas. However, the company spokesperson said that the company employs an Australian brew master and imports yeast from Australia to make the beer taste like the beer made in that country. The *Wall Street Journal* also reported that brew masters say it is difficult to make the same tasting beer in two different countries, even if the brewer replicates conditions and uses ingredients from the same source. One reason is that North American barley is considered to be more bland than the European barley.

The number one imported beer is Corona, which is still brewed in Mexico; and the number two imported beer is Heineken, which is still made in the

Netherlands. The aforementioned Beck's settlement was based on state law. There has been no lawsuit yet by the federal government; but the Federal Trade Commission could sue the beer companies based on Section 5 of the FTC Act which prohibits deceptive advertising, which can be advertising that is false or advertising that misleads the reasonable consumer into making an erroneous decision. The federal government has the power to fine wrongdoing companies, make restitution to harmed consumers, and to remove offending products from the workplace.

### *Bibliography:*

*   Gershman, Jacob and Mickle, Tripp, "Trouble Brews for 'Imported' Beers Made In America," *The Wall Street Journal*, June 25, 2015, pp. A1, A6.

### *Questions for Discussion:*

1.  Discuss the legal implications for the beer companies pursuant to the FTC legal standard? Are they in violation? If so, should they be fined, and if yes, how much?
2.  Discuss the ethical implications for the beer companies pursuant to the doctrines of Ethical Egoism, Utilitarianism, and Kantian ethics? Are they acting morally or immorally pursuant to these ethical theories? Why or why not?
3.  Regarding the Beck's settlement specifically, is it a moral one for consumers? Why or why not? And what about the lawyers?
4.  What should a socially responsible beer company be doing for the local communities where it brews its products and for society as a whole? Provide examples.
5.  How should a leader who engages in sustainable leadership respond to this brewing "brewing" controversy?

# TERMINOLOGIES

1. **Agent-Receiver Test** – an ethical test in the German philosopher Immanuel Kant's ethical principle the Categorical Imperative; an action is moral if it would be acceptable to a rational person if he or she did not know if he or she would be the "agent" (that is, doer) of the action or the receiver of the action.

2. **Categorical Imperative** – the ethics test of the German philosopher Immanuel Kant, which focuses on the form of an action and applies a three part test, and which Kant posits as the supreme and absolute test for morality.

3. **Constituency Analysis** – an examination of the impact of a corporation's actions on the company's constituent groups, also called stakeholders, in addition to the shareholders.

4. **Corporate Citizenship** – the notion of the corporation as acting legally and also morally and in a socially responsible manner.

5. **Corporate Codes of Ethics** – codes of conduct promulgated by companies as part of their corporate governance which seek to ensure that the corporation is acting legally, morally, and in a socially responsible manner.

6. **Corporate Governance** – legalistic rules from government entities which a company must obey, but also internal principles governing ethical, moral, and socially responsible conduct.

7. **Corporate Social Responsibility** – the notion that a corporation in addition to acting legally and morally should contribute to charities, be involved in civic and community affairs, and engage in sustainable environmental protection and conservation efforts.

8. **Ethical Egoism** – an ethical theory first created by the ancient Greeks that it is moral for one to advance one's self-interest, though in a prudent manner and taking a long-term prospective

9. **Ethical Relativism** – an ethical theory first created by the ancient Greeks and then developed by the Romans that morality is determined by what a society believes is moral or right.

10. **Ethics** – a branch of philosophy composed of ethical theories and principles which are used to determine morality and morals.

11. **Foreign Corrupt Practices Act** – a federal statute in the U.S. that makes bribing foreign government officials a crime, though with exceptions.

12. **"Going Green"** – a company engaging in sustainable environmental protection and conservation efforts, such as in "green buildings" and "green offices".

13. **Intrinsic Values** – also called "terminal" values; values that are good in and of themselves, such as happiness.

14. **Instrumental Values** – also called "extrinsic" values; values that are good because they are instruments, tools, or the means to achieve other things of value, for example money.

15. **Kantian Ethics** - the ethics created by the German philosopher Immanuel Kant based upon applying the Categorical Imperative to determine if an action is moral.

16. **Kingdom of Ends Test** – an ethical test in Kant's Categorical Imperative which requires that an action treat all people with dignity and respect and as worthwhile ends, as opposed to mere means, to be a moral action.

17. **Law** – rules promulgated by government entities and which are enforceable by sanctions.

18. **Leadership** – influencing and inspiring others to take action toward worthwhile and predetermined objectives.

19. **Leadership "Mindset"** – in addition to the economic and financial ramifications to an action always asking what are the legal, ethical, and social responsibility consequences.

20. **Legality** – a determination that an action is legal under the law.

21. **Morality** – the conclusion as to what is right or wrong, good or bad, or just or unjust based on the application of ethical theories and principles.

22. **"People, Planet, Profits"** – also known as the "3 P's'; a formulation of what it means to be a successful, socially responsible, and sustainable entity.

23. **Philosophy** – the study of thought and conduct, with ethics as a major branch

24. **"Reputational Capital"** – a corporate reputation of "doing good" in society which positive reputation can benefit the organization in many ways.

25. **Situational Leadership** - influencing and inspiring others by understanding their level of readiness to complete a job and adjusting one's style of management in helping them getting things successfully done using an appropriate level of task and relationship orientations.

26. **Social Entrepreneurship** – business entrepreneurship with the dual goals of successful business as well as helping to solve social and environmental problems in society.

27. **Social Responsibility** – notion that people and businesses should act beyond the law and act in an ethical and moral manner, and engage in charitable, community, and social betterment efforts, including environmental conservation and protection.

28. **Stakeholder Theory** – a notion of a corporation that is composed of many stakeholders in addition to the shareholders, including the employees, local community, and society as a whole.

29. **Stakeholder Values** – an examination expected today by a company of what the stakeholders in the business value, for example, shareholders valuing a fair return on investment, and employees valuing continued employment and a fair wage and good working conditions.

30. **Strategic Social Responsibility** – a conception of social responsibility where a firm's social responsibility efforts are prudent and reasonable and are tied to, and bolster, the company's image, brand, reputation.

31. **Sustainability** – as a "means" a form of social responsibility by engaging in environmental conservation and protection activities; an as an "ends" the result being a sustainable community, society, and planet.

32. **Sustainability Continuum** – a series of analytical steps for corporate actions ranging from economic, to legal, to moral/ethical, to socially responsible, and ultimately to sustainable.

33. **Sustainable Leadership** – leadership based on making sound decisions and adherence to the values of legality, morality, and social responsibility.

34. **"Three Value Drill"**– when contemplating a decision, in addition to the economic consequences, a business leader always asking: Is it legal? Is it moral? And what should a socially responsible firm be doing?

35. **Transactional Leadership** – influencing others toward the successful achievement of organizational goals and objectives using rewards and punishments.

36. **Transformational Leadership** – influencing others toward the successful achievement of organizational goals and objectives by inspiring, engaging and coaching others to be committed to the stated vision.

37. **"Triple Bottom Line"** – a formulation of corporate social responsibility emphasizing economic prosperity, environmental stewardship, as well as social responsibility.

38. **Universal Law Test** – another formulation of Kant's Categorical Imperative that asks if a contemplated action could be made into a universal maxim or "law".

39. **Utilitarianism** – the ethical theory created by the English philosophers and social reformers Jeremy Bentham and John Stuart Mill that bases morality on a preponderance of good consequences that are produced by an action.

40. **Values** – something that possesses worth, which can be intrinsic worth or instrumental worth.

# BIBLIOGRAHY

AACSB International (July 2013). *Spotlight: Business Schools & Ethics/Sustainability*. Retrieved on June 30, 2015 from: http://www.aacsb.edu/~/media/AACSB/Publications/Spotlights/ethics-sustainability/university-of-pittsburgh-2013.ashx

Afsharipour, Afra (Summer, 2011). Directors as Trustees of the Nation? India's Corporate Governance and Corporate Social Responsibility. *Seattle University Law Review*, Vol. 34, pp. 995-1024.

Abuznaid, S. (2006), 'Islam and management: What can be learned?', *Thunderbird International Business Review*, Vol. 48, No. 1, pp. 125-138.

Ali, Imran and Ali, Jawaria Fatima (2011). How Corporate Social Responsibility and Corporate Reputation Influence Employee Engagement. Unpublished manuscript. Available through *Munich Personal RePEc Archive*. Retrieved on June 30, 2015 from: http://mpra.ub.uni-muenchen.de/33891/

Ali, I.; Rehman, K. U.; and Akram, M. (2011). Corporate social responsibility and investor satisfaction influences on investor loyalty. *Actual Problems of Economics*, 8(122):348-357.

Ali, Abbas J. and Al-Owaihan, Abdullah (2008), 'Islamic work ethic: A critical review', *Cross Cultural Management: an International Journal*, Vol. 15, No.1, pp.5 - 19

Alsop, Ronald (January 16, 2002). Perils of Corporate Philanthropy. *The Wall Street Journal*, pp. B1, B4.

Alsop, Ronald (December 13, 2005). Recruiters Seek M.B.As Trained in Responsibility. *The Wall Street Journal*, p. B6.

Amman, W., Kerrets Makau, M., Fenton, P., Zackariasson, P., and Tripathi,(2012). *New perspectives on Management Education.* New Delhi: Excel Books.

American Law Institute (1994). 1 *Principles of Corporate Governance*, Section 2.01.

Anderson, R.C. (2000). *Mid-course correction. Toward a Sustainable Enterprise: The Interface Model.* Chelsea Green Publishing.

Andre, Rae (2012). Assessing the Accountability of the Benefit Corporation: Will This New Gray Sector Organization Enhance Corporate Social Responsibility? *Journal of Business Ethics*, Vol. 110, pp. 133-150.

Armstrong, M (2009). Handbook of Human Resource Management Practice,. Kogan Page Limited, UK

Banjo, Shelly (January 14, 2009). Next Benefit to Face Ax: Matching Gifts. *The Wall Street Journal*, pp. D1, D3.

Barnes, B. (August 19, 2013). *Six Lessons for 21st Century Leaders*. H. Huizenga School of Business and Entrepreneurship blog, Nova Southeastern

University . Retrieved on August 20, 2013 from:
http://www.huizenga.nova.edu/faculty-blog/

Barney, J. and Wright, P. (1998). On becoming strategic partner: the role of human resources in gaining competitive advantage. *Human Resource Management*, vol. 37, pp. 31-46. Available at: http://onlinelibrary.wiley.com/doi/10.1002/%28SICI%291099-050X%28199821%2937:1%3C31::AID-HRM4%3E3.0.CO;2-W/abstract

Barney, J. (1995). Looking inside for competitive advantage. *Academy of Management Executive,* vol. 9: 49-61

Bauerlein, Valerie (January 21, 2011). Pepsi Hits "Refresh" on Donor Project. *The Wall Street Journal*, p. B4.

Becker, B.E., and Huselid, M.A., Pickus, P.S. and Spratt, M.F. (1997). HR as a source of shareholder values: research and recommendations. *Human Resource Management,* 36 (1), pp. 39-47 Available at: http://onlinelibrary.wiley.com/doi/10.1002/%28SICI%291099-050X%28199721%2936:1%3C39::AID-HRM8%3E3.0.CO;2-X/abstract

Becker, B.E. and Huselid, M.A. (1998). High Performance Work Systems and Firm Performance: a synthesis of research and managerial implications. *Research in Personnel and Human Resources*, vol. 16. Retrieved on June 30, 2015 from: http://citeseerx.ist.psu.edu/viewdoc/summary?doi=10.1.1.319.7549, and at: http://www.markhuselid.com/pdfs/articles/1998_Research_in_PHRM_Paper.pdf

Bondy, Krista, Moon, Jeremy, and Matten, Dirk (2012). An Institution of Corporate Social Responsibility (CSR) in Multi-National Corporations (MNCs). *Journal of Business Ethics*, Vol. 111, pp. 281-299.

Boston University (2015). Business Education Jam. *Reimagining Business Education: A World of Ideas*.

Brady, Diane (November 12-18, 2012). Volunteerism as a Core Competency. *Bloomberg Businessweek*, pp. 53-54.

Brennan, John J. (May 10, 2010). Improving Corporate Governance: A Memo to the Board. *The Wall Street Journal*, p. A7.

Business Briefing (March 4, 2006). Wal-Mart to hire ethics watchdog. *Sun-Sentinel*, p. B1.

Business Briefing (October 26, 2011). Coke adds white, and also bears. *Sun-Sentinel*, p. 3D.

Bussey, John (October 28, 2011). Are Companies Responsible for Creating Jobs? *The Wall Street Journal*, pp. B1, B2.

Cahyandito, Martha Fani (March 2012). Corporate Social Responsibility into Millennium Development Goals is a Mere Wishful Thinking? *Journal of Management and Sustainability*, Vol. 2, No. 1, pp. 67-86.

Cavico, Frank J. (2014). *Corporate Social Responsibility and Leadership*. Davie, Florida: ILEAD Academy LLC.

Cavico, F. J., Mujtaba, B. G., Nonet, G., Rimanoczy, I., and Samuel, M. (2015). Developing a legal, Ethical, and Socially Responsible Mindset for Business Leadership. *Advances in Social Sciences Research Journal, 2(6)*, 09-26. Available at: http://scholarpublishing.org/index.php/ASSRJ

Cavico, F. J. and Mujtaba, B. G. (2014). Social Responsibility, Stakeholders, Sustainability, and Corporate Governance. Chapter 3, pp. 31-64. In *Governance in Action Globally – Strategy, Processes and Reality*, by Rossi Smith, Academic Publishers.

Cavico, F. J. and Mujtaba, B. G. (August 15, 2013). Health and Wellness Policy Ethics. *International Journal of Health Policy and Management*, 1(2), 111-113.

Cavico, F. J. and Mujtaba, B. G. (2012a). National and Global Perspectives of Corporate Social Responsibility. *International Journal of Management Sciences and Business Research*, 1(3), pp. 1-24.

Cavico, F. J. and Mujtaba, B. G. (2012b). Social Responsibility, Corporate Constituency Statutes, and the Social Benefit Corporation. *International Journal of Management and Administrative Sciences*, 1(7), pp. 21-25.

Cavico, F. J. and Mujtaba, B. G. (2013). *Business Ethics: The Moral Foundation of Effective Leadership, Management, and Entrepreneurship* (Third Edition). New York: Pearson Custom Publishing.

Cavico, F. J. and Mujtaba, B. G. (2008). *Legal Challenges for the Global Manager and Entrepreneur*. Dubuque, Iowa: Kendall-Hunt Publishing Company.

Cavico, Frank J. and Mujtaba, Bahaudin G. (2009). Making the Case for the Creation of an Academy Honesty Culture in Higher Education: Reflections and Suggestions for Reducing the Rise in Student Cheating. *American Journal of Business Education*, Vol. No. 5, pp. 75-87.

Cavico, Frank J. and Mujtaba, Bahaudin G. (2009-1). The State of Business Schools, Business Education, and Business Ethics. *Journal of Academic and Business Ethics*, Vol. 2, pp. 1-18.

Cavico, Frank J. and Mujtaba, Bahaudin, G., and McFarlane, Donovan A. (2010). *The State of Business Schools: Educational and Moral Imperatives for Market Leaders*. Davie, Florida: ILEAD Academy, LLC.

Chandler, David L. (2012, January 30). *For businesses, going green brings in greenbacks*. Retrieved from Massachusetts Institute of Technology News website: http://web.mit.edu/newsoffice/2012/manufacturing-green-0130.html

Chatterji, Aaron K., and Richman, Barak D. (Summer, 2008). Understanding the "Corporate" in Corporate Social Responsibility. *Harvard Law and Policy Review*, Vol. 2, pp. 33-48.

Christopher, John, and Bernhart, Michelle (Fall 2009). Communicate our Values: Social Responsibility as a Recruitment and Retention Strategy. *HR Florida Review*, pp. 8-12.

Chu, Kathy (April 19, 2012). Apple may polish China image. *USA Today*, p. 9A.

Clark, William H., and Babson, Elizabeth K. (2012). Business Organizations: When "Business Purpose" Disappears; How Benefit Corporations are Redefining the Purpose of Business Organizations. *William Mitchell Law Review*, Vol. 38, pp. 817-844).

Cohen, Rodgin H. and Schleyer, Glen T. (2012). Shareholder vs. Director Control Over Social Policy Matters: Conflicting Trends in Corporate Governance. *Notre Dame Journal of Law, Ethics, & Public Policy*, Vol. 26, pp. 81-124.

Cone, Tracie (October 15, 2009). IHOP egg production under fire. *Sun-Sentinel*, p. 3D.

Conlin, Michelle (November 27, 2006). More Micro, Less Soft. *Business Week*, p. 42.

Conlin, Michelle, and Hempel, Jessi (December 1, 2003). Philanthropy 2003: The Corporate Donors. *Business Week*, pp. 92-96.

Cordle, Ina Paiva (June 7, 2012). Entrepreneurs aim higher than bottom line. *Miami Herald*, pp. 1A, 5A.

Cummings, Briana (April 2012). Benefit Corporations: How to Enforce a Mandate to Promote the Public Interest. *Columbia Law Review*, Vol. 112, pp. 578-661.

Daniel, Trenton (October 22, 2010). New School, new hope for young Haitians. *The Miami Herald*. Retrieved October 22, 2010 from: http://www.miamiherald.com/2010/10/22/v-print/18885560/new-school-new-hope-for-young-haitians.

Delaney, Kevin J. (January 18, 2008). Google: From "Don't be Evil" to How to Do Good. *The Wall Street Journal*, pp. B1, B2.

Delaney, Kevin J. (October 12, 2005). Google Outlines Philanthropic Plan. *The Wall Street Journal*, p. B5.

Denning, S. (2013). The management revolution that's already happening, *Forbes*, May 30 2013. Available at: http://www.forbes.com/sites/stevedenning/2013/05/30/the-management-revolution-thats-already-happening/ (Accessed 28 September 2013).

De Roeck, Kenneth, and Delobber, Nathalie (2012). Do Environmental CSR Initiatives Serve Organizations' Legitimacy in the Oil Industry? Exploring Employees' Reactions Through Organizational Identification Theory. *Journal of Business Ethics*, Vol. 110(4), pp. 397-412.

Deskins, Michael R. (Winter, 2011). Benefit Corporation Legislation, Version 1.0 – A Breakthrough in Stakeholder Rights. *Lewis & Clark Law Review*, Vol. 15, pp. 1047-1076.

Dizik, Alina (march 4, 2010). Social Concerns Gain New Urgency. *The Wall Street Journal*, p. B10.

Du, Shullii, and Verira, Edward T. (2012). Striving for Legitimacy Through Corporate Social Responsibility: Insights from Oil Companies. *Journal of Business Ethics*, Vol. 110(4), pp. 413-427.

Eabrasu, Marian (2012). A Moral Pluralist Perspective on Corporate Social Responsibility: From Good to Controversial Practices. *Journal of Business Ethics*, Vol. 110(4), pp. 429-439.

Editorials (September 11, 2000). New Economy, New Social Contract. *Business Week*, p. 182.

Elkington, J. (1997). *Cannibals with forks: the Triple Bottom Line of 21st Century Business*. Oxford: Capstone.

Engardio, Pete (January 29, 2007). Beyond the Green Corporation. *Business Week*, pp.50-64.

EPA Green Power Partnership. (2013). *Fortune 500 Partners List*. Retrieved from http://www.epa.gov/greenpower/toplists/fortune500.htm

Executive Suite (February 6, 2006). A Social Strategist For Wal-Mart. *Business Week*, p. 11.

Flint, Joe, Branch, Shelly, and O'Connell, Vanessa (December 14, 2001). Breaking Longtime Taboo, NBC Network Plans to Accept Liquor Ads. *The Wall Street Journal*, pp. B1, B6.

*Florida Statutes* Section 607.083(3) (2011).

Foreman, Ellen (October 27, 1996). Businesses told they can be ethical and profitable. *Sun-Sentinel*, pp. 1G, 2G.

Fox, Adrienne (August 2007). Corporate Social Responsibility Pays Off. *HR Magazine*, pp. 43-47.

Garcia, Jason (September 30, 2005). 1 Million Volunteers to Visit Disney for Free. *Sun-Sentinel*, Money, pp. 1-2.

Garriga, E. and Melé, D. (2004). Corporate social responsibility theories: Mapping the territory. *Journal of Business Ethics* 53(1-2), pp.51-71.

Gelter, Martin (Spring, 2011). Taming or Protecting the Modern Corporation? Shareholder – Stakeholder Debates in a Comparative Light. *New York University Journal of Law & Business*, Vol. 7, pp. 641-740.

George, Bill (September 13-19, 2010). Executive Pay: Rebuilding Trust in an Era of Rage. *Bloomberg Businessweek*, p. 56.

Givray, Henry S. (September 3, 2007). When CEOs Aren't Leaders. *Business Week*, p. 102.

GlaxoSmithKline (2005). Corporate Responsibility Report 2005. Retrieved January 28, 2007 from: http://www.gsk.com/respnsibility/cr_report_2005.

Goodman, Cindy Krischer (November 8, 2006). Volunteering through work isn't always so voluntary. *The Miami Herald*, pp. 1C, 5C.

Gore, Al and Blood, David (July 24, 2010). Toward Sustainable Capitalism. *The Wall Street Journal*, p. 21.

Gupta, Atul (July/August, 2012). Sustainable Competitive Advantage in Service Corporations. *The Journal of Applied Business Research*, Vol. 28, No. 4, pp.735-42.

Guthrie, W.K.C. (1988). *The Sophists*. Great Britain: Cambridge University Press.

Hai-yan, He, Amerzaga, Teodoro Rafael Wendlandt, and Silva, Beatriz Ochoa (March 2012). Corporate Social Responsibility Perspectives and Practices in Chinese Companies: A Brief Overview on Environment, Consumers and External Communication. *Journal of Management and Sustainability*, Vol. 2, No. 1, pp. 57-86.

Harish, N. (May 2012). Corporate Social Responsibility Practices in Indian Companies: A Study. *International Journal of Management, IT and Engineering,* Vol. 2, Issue 5, pp. 519-36.

*Harvard Business Review* (April 2015). "Leadership: Measuring the Return on Character." Retrieved May 17, 2015 from: http://hbr.org/2015/04/measurng-the-return-on-character.

Harrington, Alexandra R. (2011/2012). Protecting Workers' Rights in a Post-Wisconsin World: Strategies for Organizing and Action in an Era of Diminished Resources and Embattled Unions: Corporate Social Responsibility, Globalization, the Multinational Corporation, and Labor: An Unlikely Alliance. *Albany Law Review*, Vol. 75, pp. 481-508.

Hasnas, John (2013). Whiter Stakeholder Theory? A Guide for the Perplexed Revisited. *Journal of Business Ethics*, Vol. 112, pp. 47-57.

Haymore, Steven J. (May, 2011). Publicly Oriented Companies: B Corporations and the Delaware Stakeholder Provision Dilemma. *Vanderbilt Law Review*, Vo. 64, pp. 1311-1342.

Heineman, Jr., Ben W. (June 28, 2005). Are You a Good Corporate Citizen? *The Wall Street Journal*, p. B2.

Hemlock, Doreen (March 11, 2007). It's all good: Social awareness now a corporate requirement. *Sun-Sentinel,* Business and Money, pp. 1E, 2E.

Hempel, Jessi, and Gard, Lauren (November 29, 2004). Philanthropy 2004: The Corporate Donors. *Business Week*, pp. 100-104.

Hersey, P. & Campbell, R. (2004). *Leadership: A Behavioral Science Approach.* California: Leadership Studies Publishing.

Hersey, P., Blanchard, K., and Johnson, D. (2001). *Management of Organizational Behavior*. 8th ed. Prentice Hall.

Higgens, Alexander G. (June 21, 2001). Coca-Cola to join AIDs fight in Africa. *The Miami Herald*, p. 4C.

Hiltrop, J.M. (1995). The changing psychological contract: the human resource challenge of the 1990s. *European Management Journal, vol. 13, No. 3, pp.* 286–294

Holme, Lord and Watts, Richard (January 2000). Making Good Business Sense. *The World Business Council for Sustainable Development. Pp. 01-19. Retrieved on June 30, 2015 from: http://www.wbcsd.org/web/publications/csr2000.pdf*

Homes, Stanley (September 9, 2002). For Coffee Growers, Not Even a Whiff of Profits. *Business Week*, p. 110.

Horney, K. (1951). Neurosis and Human Growth: The Struggle Toward Self-Realization. London: Routledge and Kegan Paul

Jacobs, Michael (April 24, 2009). How Business Schools Have Failed Business. *The Wall Street Journal, p. A13.*

Jo, Hoje, and Na, Haejung (2012). Does CSR Reduce Firm Risk? Evidence from Controversial Industry Sectors. *Journal of Business Ethics*, Vol. 110(4), pp. 441-456.

John, Leisha (2015), Director of Environmental Sustainability for Ernst & Young, Speaker at *Sustainability 101 Lunch Series*. The H. Wayne Huizenga School of Business, Nova Southeastern University, April 21, 2015.

Kaufman-Rosen, Leslie (October 17, 1994). Being Cruel to be Kind. *Newsweek*, p. 51.

Kedge Business School (2009-2010). *Responsible Managers, Valuing Diversity.* Available at: http://www.euromed-management.com/en/RESEARCH%20%2526%20VISION/Responsible%20Managers (Accessed 28 September 2013).

Kickul, Jill, Terjesen, Siri, Bacq, Sophie, and Griffiths, Mark (September, 2012). Social Business Education: An Interview with Nobel Laureate Muhammad Yunus. The Academy of Management. Learning & Education, Vol. 11, No. 3, pp. 453-462.

Kramer, M. R. (2011). Shared Value vs. Don't be Evil. *Harvard Business Review*, Vol. 89, No. 7/8, pp. 18-19.

Kumar, P.S.S., Kuberudu, B., and Krishna, Srinivasa (January, 2011). Corporate Social Responsibility – Public Sensitivity. *Proficient*, pp. 7-13.

Lacovara, Christopher (2011). Strange Creatures: A Hybrid Approach to Fiduciary Duty in Benefit Corporations. *Columbia Business Law Review*, Vol. 2011, pp. 815-861.

Lawrence, Thomas, Phillips, Nelson, and Tracey, Paul (September, 2012). Educating Social Entrepreneurs and Social Innovators. The Academy of Management. *Learning & Education*, Vol. 11, No. 3, pp. 319-323.

Leisner, Richard M. (November, 1990). Florida's New Business Corporation Act. *The Florida Bar Journal*, pp. 9-15.

Liedtke, Michael (May 13, 2004). Gap vows to end plant abuses. *The Miami Herald*, pp. 1C, 4C.

Lindgreen, Adam, Maon, Francios, Reast, Jon, and Yani-De-Soriano (2012). Corporate Social Responsibility in Controversial Industry Sectors. *Journal of Business Ethics*, Vol. 110(4), pp. 393-95.

Lindorff, Margaret, Prior, Elizabeth Jonson, and McGuire, Linda (2012), Strategic Corporate Responsibility in Controversial Industry Sectors: The Social Value of Harm Minimization. *Journal of Business Ethics*, Vol. 110 (4), pp. 457-467.

Linn, Allison. (2007, April 18). *Corporations find business case for going green.* Retrieved from NBC News website: http://www.nbcnews.com/id/17969124/ns/business-going_green/t/corporations-find-business-case-going-green/#.UdtRrvlTBrs

Loten, Angus (January 19, 2012). With New Law, Profits Take Back Seat. *The Wall Street Journal*, pp. B1, B5.

Mackey, John, and Sisodia, Raj (2013). *Conscious Capitalism*. Boston: Harvard Business Review Press.

Maggins, Anastasia, and Tsaklanganos, Angelos A. (July/August, 2012). Predicting the Corporate Social Responsibility of Limited Liability Companies in Greece Using Market Variables. *The Journal of Applied Business Research*, Vol. 28, No. 4, pp. 661-671.

Marketing (August 8-12, 2012). Do-Gooder Retailing Goes Mainstream. *Business Week*, pp. 22-23.

Marx, Karl (1867). Capital vol. 1, trans. Ben Fowkes, New York: Vintage Books.

Mawdudi, Abul Aala (1996). The Making of Islamic Revivalism. New York: OUP.

McClatchy-Tribune News April 11, 2011). Socially responsible investing: Websites highlight how to do it. *Sun-Sentinel*, Money, p. 1.

McConnell, Beth (November 20, 2006). HR implements corporate social responsibility globally. *Society for Human Resource Management HR News*.

McKay, Betsy (March 15, 2007). Why Coke Aims to Slake Global Thirst for Safe Water. *The Wall Street Journal*, pp. B1, B2.

Merrick, Amy (May 12, 2004). Gap Offers Unusual Look at Factory Conditions. *The Wall Street Journal*, pp. A1, A12.

Minnesota Pollution Control Agency. (n.d.). *Become a paper-less office*. Retrieved from http://156.98.19.245/paper/Minnesota Pollution Control Agency. (n.d.). *Reducing waste in the workplace*. Retrieved from http://156.98.19.245/workplace/

*Minnesota Statutes* Section 302A.251(5) (2011).

Millward, L.J. and L.J. Hopkins 'Psychological contracts, organizational and job commitment,' *Journal of Applied Social Psychology* (1998) 28: 16–31.

Mickels, Alissa (Winter, 2009). Beyond Corporate Social Responsibility. *Hastings International and Comparative Law Journal*, Vol. 32, pp. 271-300.

Miller, Toyah L., Grimes, Matthew G., McMullen, Jeffrey S., and Vogus, Timothy J. (2012). Venturing for Others with Heart and Head: How Compassion Encourages Social Entrepreneurship. *Academy of Management Review*, Vol. 37, No. 4, pp. 616-640.

Millon, David (Fall, 2011). Two Models of Corporate Social Responsibility. *Wake Forest Law Review*, Vol. 46, pp. 523-35.

Mintzberg, H. (2004). *Managers not MBA*. San Francisco: Berret-Koehler.

Mizruchi, Mark S., and Hirschman, Daniel (Summer, 2010). The Modern Corporation as Social Construction. *Seattle University Law Review*, Vol. 33, pp. 1065-1105.

Mohrman, S. A., O'Toole, J., and Lawler III, E. E., editors, (2015). *Corporate Stewardship: Achieving Sustainable Effectiveness*. Greenleaf Publishing: UK.

Mujtaba, B. G. (2014). *Managerial Skills and Practices for Global Leadership*. ILEAD Academy: Florida.

Mujtaba, B. G. (2014). *Capitalism and its Challenges Across Borders (edited)*. Florida: ILEAD Academy.

Mujtaba, B. G. (2007). *Mentoring Diverse Professionals (2nd edition)*. Llumina Press. Davie, Florida, United States.

Mujtaba, B. G. and Cavico, F. J. (2013). A Review of Employee Health and Wellness Programs in the United States. *Public Policy and Administration Research*, 3(4), 01-15.

Mujtaba, B. G., and Cavico, F. J. (2013). Corporate Social Responsibility and Sustainability Model for Global Firms. *Journal of Leadership, Accountability and Ethics*, Vol. 10(1), pp. 58-76.

Mujtaba, B.G., Cavico, F.J., and Chen, L. (2010). Ethics in Education: A Must for Integrity. *MBA Review*, Vol. IX, No. 1, pp. 18-22.

Mujtaba, B. G. and McCartney, T. (2010). *Managing Workplace Stress and Conflict amid Change, 2nd edition*. ILEAD Academy: Florida.

Mujtaba, B.G., Cavico, F.J.. and Acheraporn, P. (2012). Corporate Social Responsibility and Globalization. *Proceedings of the 17th International Conference of Asia Pacific Decision Sciences Institute (APDSI)*, Chaing Mai, Thailand. July 22-26, 2012.

Mujtaba, B. G. and Preziosi, R. C (2006). *Adult Education in Academia: Recruiting and Retaining Extraordinary Facilitators of learning*. 2nd Edition. Information Age Publishing: Greenwich.

Munch, Steven (Winter, 2012). Improving the Benefit Corporation: How Traditional Governance Mechanisms Can Enhance the Innovative New Business Form. *Northwestern Journal of Law and Social Policy*, Vol.7, pp. 170-225.

Naik, Gautam (September 6, 2002). Glaxo to Cut Prices in Poor Countries. *The Wall Street Journal*, p. B1.

Nonet, G. (2013). Responsible Management and Business Schools: Analysis of the Schools Strategy and the Education / Management Responsable et Business Schools: Une analyse par les strategies d'etablissement et par les projets pedagogiques, PhD defended on November 27th 2013, Montpellier University, France.

Nonet, G., Meijs, L., Kassel, K. (2014). Business School and Responsible Management: A long Road to Freedom, *NITTE Management Review Special ISSUE on Management Education* 8(2) December 2014, pp.1-10.

O'Connell, Vanessa (January 3, 2002). Landmark TV Liquor Ad Created by D.C. Insiders. *The Wall Street Journal*, pp. B1, B3.

O'Leary-Kelly, A.M. and J.A. Schenk (1999) '*An examination of the development and consequences of psychological contracts'*. Paper presented at the annual Meeting of the Academy of Management, Chicago.

Office Depot. (n.d.). *Top 20 Ways to Go Green at Work (and Save the University Money!)*. Retrieved from University of Washington website: http://www.washington.edu/admin/stores/eprocurement/office/green.pdf

Page, Antony, and Katz, Robert A. (Summer, 2011). Is Social Enterprise the New Corporate Social Responsibility. *Seattle University Law Review*, Vol. 34, pp. 1351-1384.

Paul, Sudhakar T. (January, 2012). Green Business or Sustainable Business: A Triple Bottom-line Approach. *Proficient*, pp. 78-87.

Pfeffer, J. (1995). Competitive advantage through people: Unleashing the power of the workforce. Boston, Harvard Business School Press.

Podsada, Janice (October 13, 2011). Handicrafts headed to Wal-Mart's website. *Sun-Sentinel*, p. 4D.

Porter, M.E. and Kramer, M.R. (2011). Creating Shared Value – How to Reinvent Capitalism and Unleash a Wave of Innovation and Growth. *Harvard Business Review*, Vol. 89, No. 1/2, pp. 63-77.

Porter, M.E. and Kramer, M.R. (2006). Strategy and Society: The Link between Competitive Advantage and Corporate Social Responsibility. *Harvard Business Review*, Vol. 84, pp. 78-92.

Pressman, Aaron (October 24, 2005). Activist Funds Make Waves. *Business Week*, p. 124.

Rashid, A.T. and Rahman, M. (2009). Making Profit to Solve Developmental Problems: The Case of Telenor AS and the Village Phone Program in Bangladesh. *Journal of Marketing Management*, Vol. 25, No. 9, pp. 1049-60.

Reich, Robert (September 10, 2007). It's Not Business' Business. *Business Week*, p. 86.

Reiser, Dana Brakman (Fall, 2011). Benefit Corporations – A Sustainable Form of Organization? *Wake Forest Law Review*, Vol. 46, pp. 591-620.

Resor, Felicia R. (2012). Benefit Corporation Legislation. *Wyoming Law Review*, Vol. 12, pp. 91-119.

Richards, Bill (May 13, 1998). Nike to Increase Minimum Age in Asia for New Hirings, Improve Air Quality. *The Wall Street Journal*, p. B10.

Rimanoczy, I. B. (2010). Business leaders committing to and fostering sustainability initiatives. *Doctoral dissertation*. Teachers College, Columbia University.

Rimanoczy, I. (2013). *Big Bang Being: Developing the Sustainability Mindset.* Sheffield, UK: Greenleaf Publishing.

Rimanoczy, Isabel (May 1, 2015). Sustainability: A Matter of Soul. *Generation Change, The Huffington Post*. Retrieved May 12, 2015 from: http://www.huffingtonpost.com/isabel-rimanoczy-edd-/sustainability.

Robinson, S.L. (December 1996). 'Trust and breach of the psychological contract', *Administrative Science Quarterly,* () 41, No. 4, pp. 574-599. Available at: http://www.jstor.org/stable/2393868?seq=1#page_scan_tab_contents

Roche (2007). Sustainable Humanitarian Aid. Retrieved January 28, 2007 from: http://www.roche.com/home.sustainability/sus_csoc-resp/sus.

Rodgers, T.J. (April 30, 1997). Corporations' social responsibility: Increase profits. *The Miami Herald*, p. 11A.

Rodinson, Maxime (1973). Islam and Capitalism. New York: Pantheon Books.

Rogers, Carl R. (1961). On Becoming a Person. Boston: Houghton Mifflin.

Ronald McDonald House Charities of South Florida (February 9, 2012). Celebrating Thirty Years. *Sun-Sentinel*, Special Advertising Section.

Ryan, A., Tilbury, D., Parkes, C., Blewitt, J. (2011). Ignorance was bliss, now I'm not ignorant and that is far more difficult - Transdisciplinary learning and reflexivity in responsible management education. *Journal of Global Responsibility* 2(2), pp. 206-221.

Sadler, Philip (2010). *Consumption, Demand, and the Poverty Penalty*. Surrey, England: Gower Applied Research.

Salcedo, Diandra (2015). Director of Marketing and Community Relations for Whole Foods Market. Speaker at *Sustainability 101 Lunch Series*. The H. Wayne Huizenga School of Business, Nova Southeastern University, April 21, 2015.

Sampson, Hannah (June 5, 2015). Carnival launches "social impact travel" brand. *Miami Herald*, pp. 1C, 3C.

Sauser, Jr., William I. (2008). Regulating Ethics and Business: Review and Recommendations. SAM: Management in Practice, Vol. 12, No. 4, pp.1-7.

Schneitz, Karen E., and Epstein, Marc J. (Winter 2005). Exploring the Financial Value of a Reputation for Corporate Social Responsibility During a Crisis. *Corporate Reputation Review*, Vol.7, No. 4, pp. 327-45.

Schoops., Mark (January 14, 2004). HIV Test Makers Agree to Discounts for Poorer Nations. *The Wall Street Journal*, pp. B1, B2.

Schuler, Douglas A., and Cording. Margaret (2006). A Corporate Social Performance-Corporate Financial Performance Behavior Model for Consumers. *Academy of Management Review*, Vol. 31, No. 3, pp. 540-58.

Schwab, Klaus (January 15, 2010). Bank Bonuses and Communitarian Spirit. *The Wall Street Journal*, p. A19.

Shellenburger, Sue (October 13, 2005). Employers Begin to Provide Assistance for Parents of Children with Disabilities. *The Wall Street Journal*, p. D1.

Sherman, Richard W. (July/August, 2012). The Triple Bottom Line: The Reporting of "Doing Well" & "Doing Good." *The Journal of Applied Business Research*, Vol. 28, No. 4, pp. 672-682.

Shillington, Patty (June 16, 2008). Investors do well doing good. *The Miami Herald*, Business Monday, p. 13.

Smalley, Suzanne (December 3, 2007). Ben and Jerry's Bitter Crunch. Newsweek, p. 50.

Spector, Jonathan (2012). The Sustainability Imperative and Governance: Understanding a New Frontier in Corporate Board Oversight. *Notre Dame Journal of Law, Ethics, and Public Policy*, Vol. 26, pp. 39-44.

Swallow, Lisa, & Furniss, Jerry. (2011). *Green Business Reducing Carbon Footprint Cuts Costs and Provides Opportunities.* Retrieved from Bureau of Business and Economic Research, the University of Montana website: http://www.bber.umt.edu/pubs/MBQ/greenbusinessarticle.pdf

Taqiuddin, al-Nabahani (2002). The economic System of Islam. New Delhi: Milli Publications.

Tasker, Fred (September 23, 2010). AIDS, HIV patients getting help from pharmaceutical companies. *The Miami Herald*, p. 5B.

Tasker, Fred (January 20, 2011). Funding gap threatens AIDS drug help. *The Miami Herald*, p. 5B.

Taylor, Celia R. (Summer, 2011). Berle and Social Businesses: A Consideration. *Seattle University Law Review*, Vol. 34, pp. 1501-20.

Tellus Institute. (2002). *Greening Your Products: Good for the environment, good for your bottom line.* Retrieved from US Environmental Protection Agency website: http://www.epa.gov/epp/pubs/jwod_product.pdf

The Environment Agency (n.d.). *Climate Change Agreements Scheme.* Retrieved from http://www.environment-agency.gov.uk/business/topics/pollution/136236.aspx

Tyagi, R.K. (November, 2011). A Conceptual Study of Corporate Social Responsibility and Its Persuasion on Employees. *Proficient*, pp. 2837.

Udgata, Jitarani and Das, Sarita (March 2012). Social Entrepreneurship: Challenges and Opportunities. *Tenecia Journal of Management Studies*, Vol. 6, No. 2, pp. 50-57.

Uwalomwa, Uwuigbe and Egbide, Ben-Caleb (March 2012). Corporate Social Responsibility Disclosures in Nigeria: A Study of Listed Financial and Non-Financial Firms. *Journal of Management and Sustainability*, Vol. 2, No. 1, pp. 160-69.

Vago, Thomas (2015), Director of Operations at Hilton Ft. Lauderdale Beach Resort, Speaker at *Sustainability 101 Lunch Series*. The H. Wayne Huizenga School of Business, Nova Southeastern University, April 21, 2015. Waddock, S. (2007). Leadership integrity in a fractured knowledge world. *Management learning & education,* 6(4), pp.543-557.

Wang, Heli and Qian, Cuili (2012). Corporate Philanthropy and Corporate Financial Performance: The Roles of Stakeholder Response and Political Access. *Academy of Management Journal*, Vol. 54, No. 6, pp. 1159-1181.

Windham, Christopher (March 29, 2004). J&J to Give Away New AIDS Drug. *The Wall Street Journal*, p. B6.

Windsor, D. (2006). Corporate social responsibility: Three key approaches. *Journal of Management Studies* 43(1), pp.93-114.

Workplace Visions (2007). Social Responsibility and HR Strategy. *Society for Human Resource Management*, No. 2, pp. 2-8.

World Bank Institute (2007). Internet Course: "CSR and Sustainable Competitiveness." Retrieved January 27, 2007 from: www.infoworldbank.org/etools/wbi_learning/index.

World Commission on Environment and Development. (1987). *Our Common Future, Report of the World Commission on Environment and Development.* Published as Annex to General Assembly Document

A/42/427, *Development and International Co-operation: Environment*, August 2, 1987.

World Wide Fund for Nature. (n.d.). *How to reduce paper consumption in your office (and save money at the same time!).* Retrieved from http://awsassets.panda.org/downloads/final_paper_saving_tips_1.pdf

Yolles, Y. and Fink, G. (2014). The Sustainability of Sustainability. *Business Systems Review*, 3(2), 01-32. Website: https://www.academia.edu/14281687/The_Sustainability_of_Sustainability?auto=download&campaign=upload_email

# Author Biography

*Frank J. Cavico* is a Professor of Business Law and Ethics at the H. Wayne Huizenga College of Business and Entrepreneurship of Nova Southeastern University in Ft. Lauderdale, Florida. He has been involved in an array of teaching responsibilities, at the undergraduate, master's and doctoral levels, encompassing such subject matter areas as business law, government regulation of business, constitutional law, administrative law and ethics, labor law and labor relations, health care law, and business ethics. In 2000, he was awarded the Excellence in Teaching Award by the Huizenga School; and in 2007, he was awarded the Faculty Member of the Year Award by the Huizenga School of Business and Entrepreneurship; and in 2012 he was again honored by the Huizenga School as Faculty Member of the Year. Frank Cavico holds a J.D. from the St. Mary's University School of Law and an LL.M from the University of San Diego, School of Law; and is a member of the Florida and Texas Bar Associations. He is the author and co-author of several books and numerous law review and management journal articles.


*Bahaudin G. Mujtaba* is Professor of International Management and Human Resources at the H. Wayne Huizenga College of Business and Entrepreneurship of Nova Southeastern University in Ft. Lauderdale, Florida. Bahaudin is the author and coauthor of twenty professional and academic books dealing with management, diversity, business ethics, and cross-cultural management, as well as over 300 academic journal articles. During the past thirty years he has had the pleasure of working with management and human resource professionals in the United States, Brazil, Bahamas, Afghanistan, Pakistan, St. Lucia, Grenada, Malaysia, Japan, Vietnam, China, India, Thailand, and Jamaica. This diverse exposure has provided him many insights in ethics, culture, and international management from the perspectives of different firms, people groups, and countries. Bahaudin can be reached at: mujtaba@nova.edu

# Index

| Y |
|---|

Yunus, 125

| Z |
|---|

Zuckerberg, 35